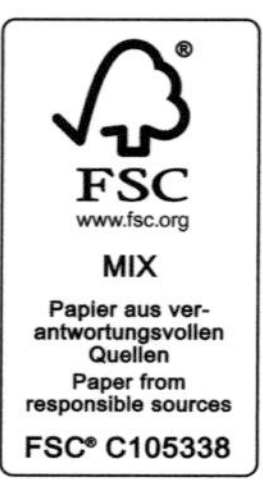

Bibliografische Information der Deutschen Nationalbibliothek: Die Deutsche Nationalbibliothek verzeichnet diese Publikation in der Deutschen Nationalbibliografie; detaillierte bibliografische Daten sind im Internet über dnb.dnb.de abrufbar.

Herstellung und Verlag: BoD – Books on Demand, Norderstedt

ISBN: 9783753441306

Das Zine BLAST ist im Rahmen der Lehrveranstaltung für künstlerische Fotografie von Sascha Reichstein am Institut für künstlerisches Lehramt der Akademie der Bildenden Künste Wien im Wintersemester 2020/21 entstanden.

Die zurzeit herrschende Situation der Corona-Pandemie, des Klimawandels und des gesellschaftlichen wie politischen Umbruchs, lässt uns auf die Zeit vor ca. 100 Jahren zurückblicken, die von Unsicherheit, Arbeitslosigkeit sowie revolutionären Bewegungen innerhalb der Künste geprägt war.

Historisch betrachtet gab es im letzten Jahrhundert unterschiedliche Phasen der Verunsicherung. Der Titel unseres Zines bezieht sich auf die im Juli 1914 erschienene, erste Ausgabe der Zeitschrift „BLAST", die lediglich zwei Mal erschienen ist und von den ‚Vortizisten', allen voran Percy Wyndham Lewis und Ezra Pound, herausgegeben worden ist. Künstlerische Positionen wurden klar und kämpferisch formuliert. Heute befinden wir uns erneut in einer ähnlichen gesellschaftlichen Situation, die sowohl demokratische Strukturen als auch gesellschaftliche und soziale Gewohnheiten ins wanken bringt und deren Stabilität hinterfragen lässt. Der Begriff ‚Vortizismus' wurde unter anderen von dem amerikanischen Dichter Ezra Pound geprägt und bedeutete im wörtlichen Sinne ‚Wirbel' oder ‚Strudel'. Wyndham Lewis sah „im Zentrum des Strudels einen großen ruhigen Ort, an dem alle Energie konzentriert ist".

Ein Zine mit Beiträgen von:
Lisa Achammer, Jacob Bartmann, Jessica Koppa, Elke Leithner, Johanna Schlager, Victor Thiery, Svenja Zewe

Etwas Unsichtbares stellt
die Welt auf den Kopf

Unvermittelt wurden wir in eine Zeit des Umbruchs, der Unsicherheit und somit der Möglichkeit des Überdenkens unserer vermeintlichen Realität katapultiert. Gewohnheiten und strukturelle Bedingungen werden verändert und greifen in unser privates und öffentliches Leben ein. Das Bewusstsein, dass die Errungenschaften unserer demokratischen Gesellschaften nicht uneingeschränkt vorhanden sind, rückt in den Mittelpunkt. Wir realisieren, dass wir dafür zu sorgen, ja zu kämpfen haben, diese Strukturen und Möglichkeiten zu erhalten. Es gilt eine gesamtgesellschaftliche Schärfung der Sinne zu beleben und zu etablieren. Unerwartet ist Sicherheit auch in unserer westlichen Welt nichts mehr, was im Außen existiert. Die Gewissheit unserer Werte, Gewohnheiten und Selbstverständlichkeiten wurden ins Wanken gebracht.

Welche Bilder können die momentanen politischen und sozialen Gegebenheiten veranschaulichen? Welche Möglichkeiten bieten sich uns als bildenden Künstler_innen innerhalb einer künstlerischen Auseinandersetzung auf gesellschaftliche Veränderungen zu reagieren? Durch die Summe und Schnittmenge unserer Einzelpositionen, versuchten wir, ein kollektives Empfinden der Gegenwart darzustellen. Unsere fotografischen Bilder sollen das Unsichtbare sichtbar machen.

Sascha Reichstein und StudentInnen

The zine BLAST was created as part of the course for fine-art photography held by Sascha Reichstein at the Institute for Education in the Arts at the Academy of Fine Arts Vienna during the 2020/21 winter term.

The current situation is dominated by the overarching corona pandemic, climate change, as well as social and political upheaval. This inspired us to look back at the time 100 years ago, which was characterized by insecurity and unemployment, but also revolutionary movements in the arts.

Historically, the last century was shaped by different phases of insecurity. The title of our zine refers back to the first issue of the literary magazine "BLAST", which was published in July 1914. The magazine was edited by the "Vorticists", headed by Percy Wyndham Lewis and Ezra Pound. In total, only two issues of this short-lived magazine were published. Artistic positions were formulated in a imperious and poignant way. Today we find ourselves in a similar situation; democratic structures as well as social and societal habits are shaken, which makes us question their stability. Among others, the American poet Ezra Pound coined the term "Vorticism", which is derived from Latin and translates as "whirl". Wyndham Lewis found "at the center of the vortex a great calm place where all energy is concentrated."

A zine with contributions from:
Lisa Achammer, Jacob Bartmann, Jessica Koppa, Elke Leithner, Johanna Schlager, Victor Thiery, Svenja Zewe

Something invisible turns the world upside down

Without warning, we have been catapulted into a time of upheaval and uncertainty which creates the possibility of rethinking our reality. New, structural interventions impact our habits and have changed our private and public lives.
The awareness that achievements of our democratic societies are, in fact, not irrevocable made its way into public consciousness. We realize that we have to take action in order to maintain these structures and opportunities. It is necessary to achieve a sharpening of the senses in society as a whole. Unexpectedly, even in the Western World, certainty no longer exists of our values, habits and self-evident facts has been shaken. Images can illustrate current political and social realities? Which tools make such a reaction to social change possible within an artistic confrontation? In this endeavour, we adopted subjective views, a visual exploration of individual realities, without aiming at objective representation. Through our photographic images we try to make the invisible visible.
This zine brings together a diversity of artistic approaches and expressions of visual thoughts.

Sascha Reichstein and Students

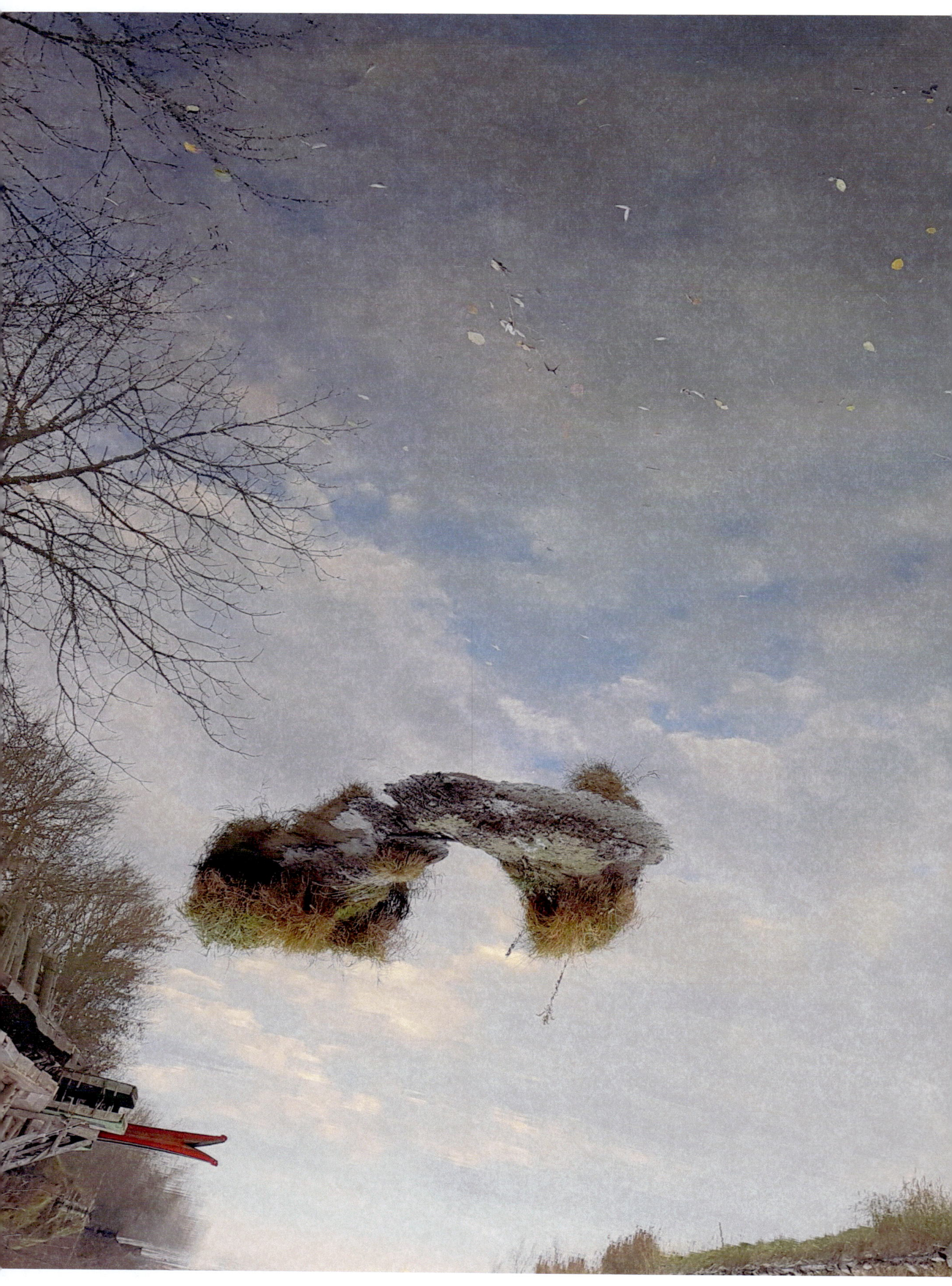

VICTOR THIERY

Dream scapes

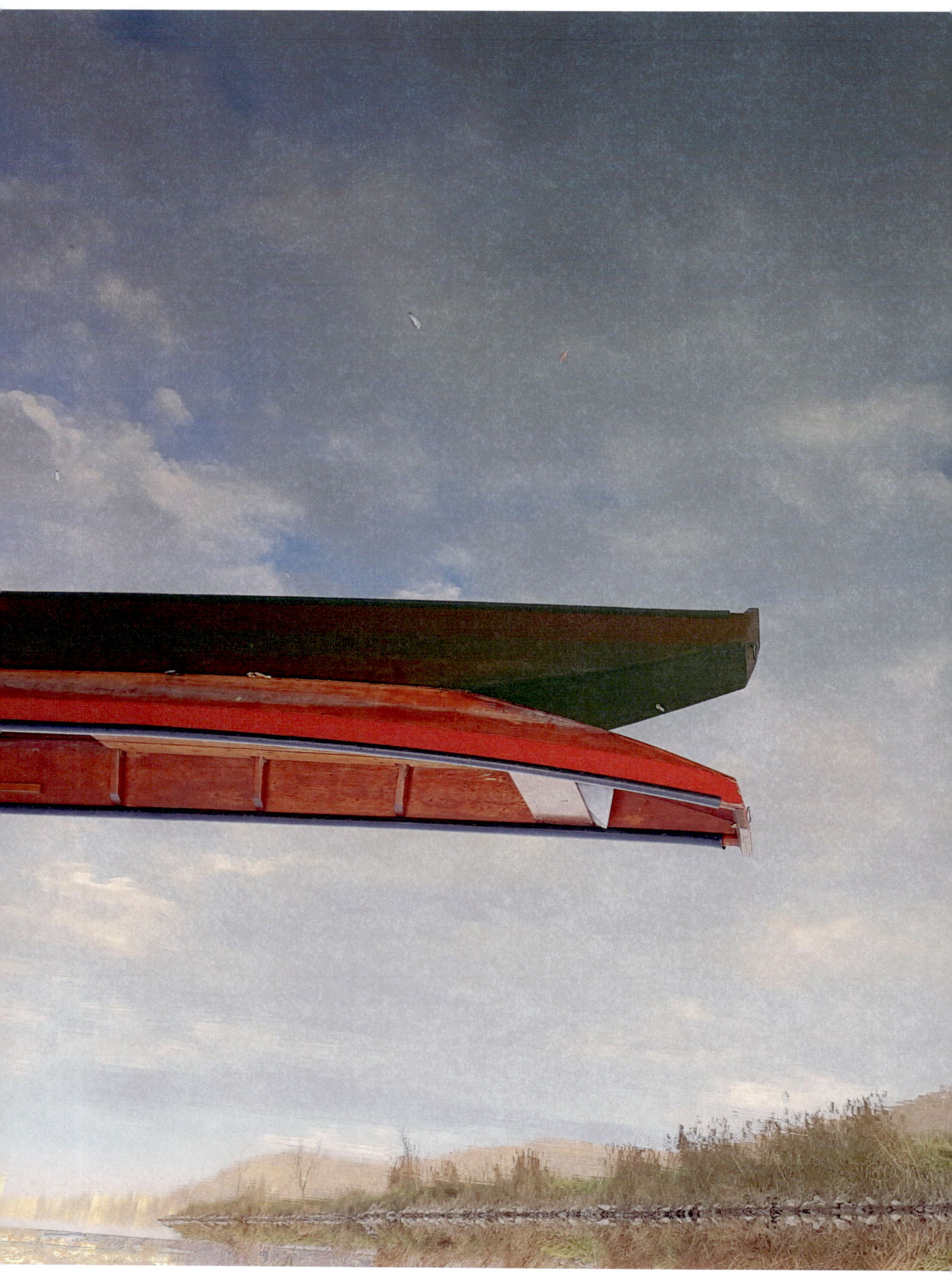

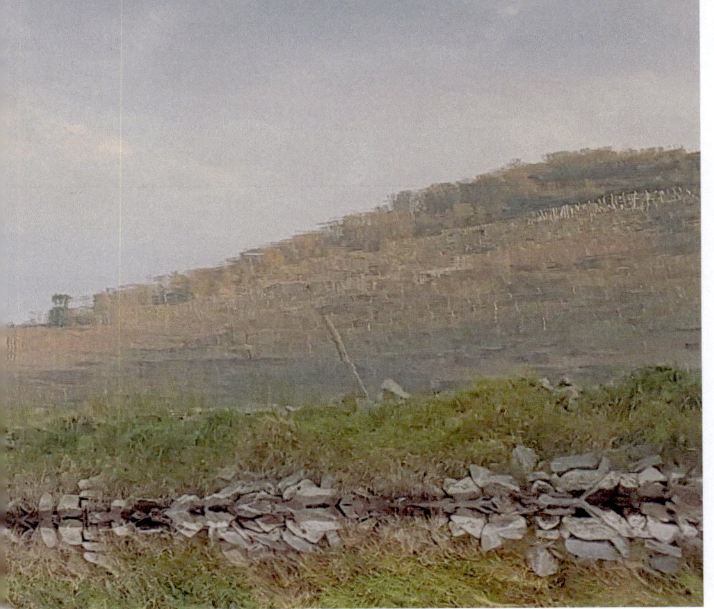

Sucked in by the stillness of the surface,
reflection becomes reality
as lines dissolve into each other.
Senses twist and twirl,
trying to make sense of the implausible
until my mind dives in
and through to an other side.
There is potential in this
sense of disorientation.
It provides an opportunity to refocus:
breaking down expectations

of what is supposed to happen
and conjuring up what
might possibly be.

New thoughts and ideas surface
as I gaze beyond and get lost
in my own mind.

A sense of wonder surrounds
and comforts me.
Offering an escape in times of unrest,
when everything seems to be calm
and collected but, in fact is not.

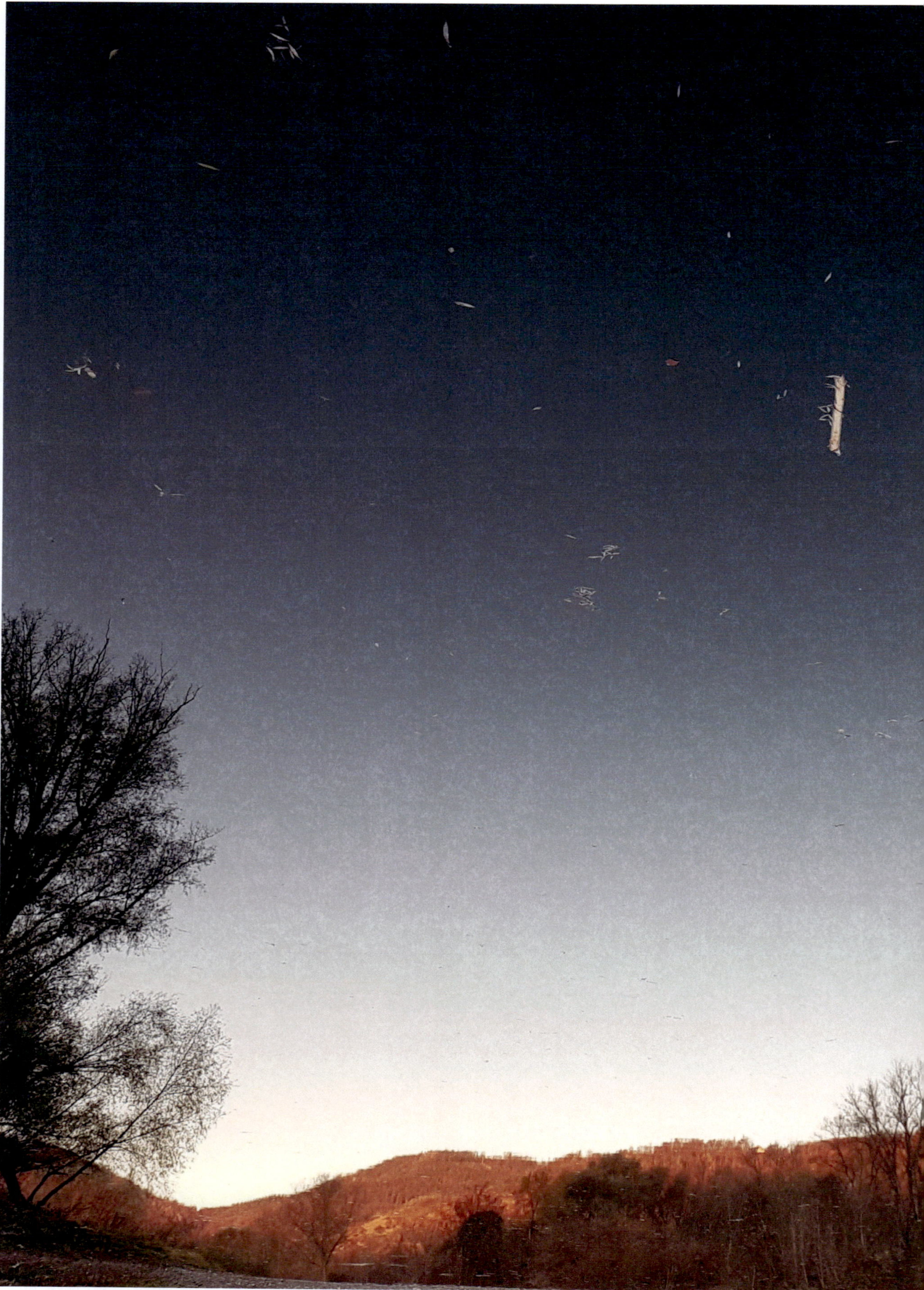

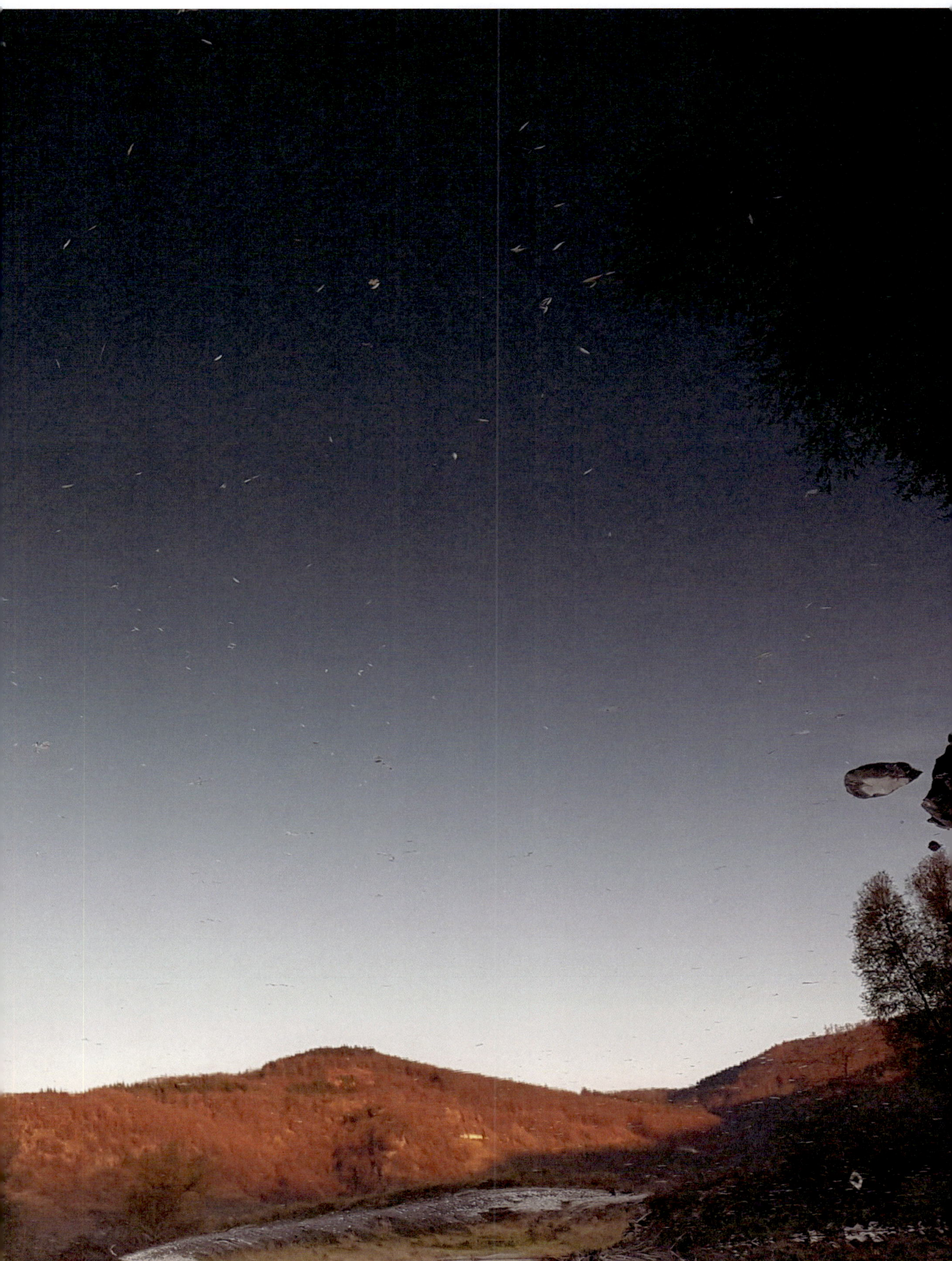

JOHANNA SCHLAGER

In meiner Ferne

In meiner Ferne
durchwandere ich Hügel,
die der Schatten bloß
in seinen Armen hält.
Ich umziehe sie in Kreisen,
zeige mir Blöße und
verjage das Wilde.
In meiner Ferne finde ich Nähe
und mein Körper sein Fleisch.

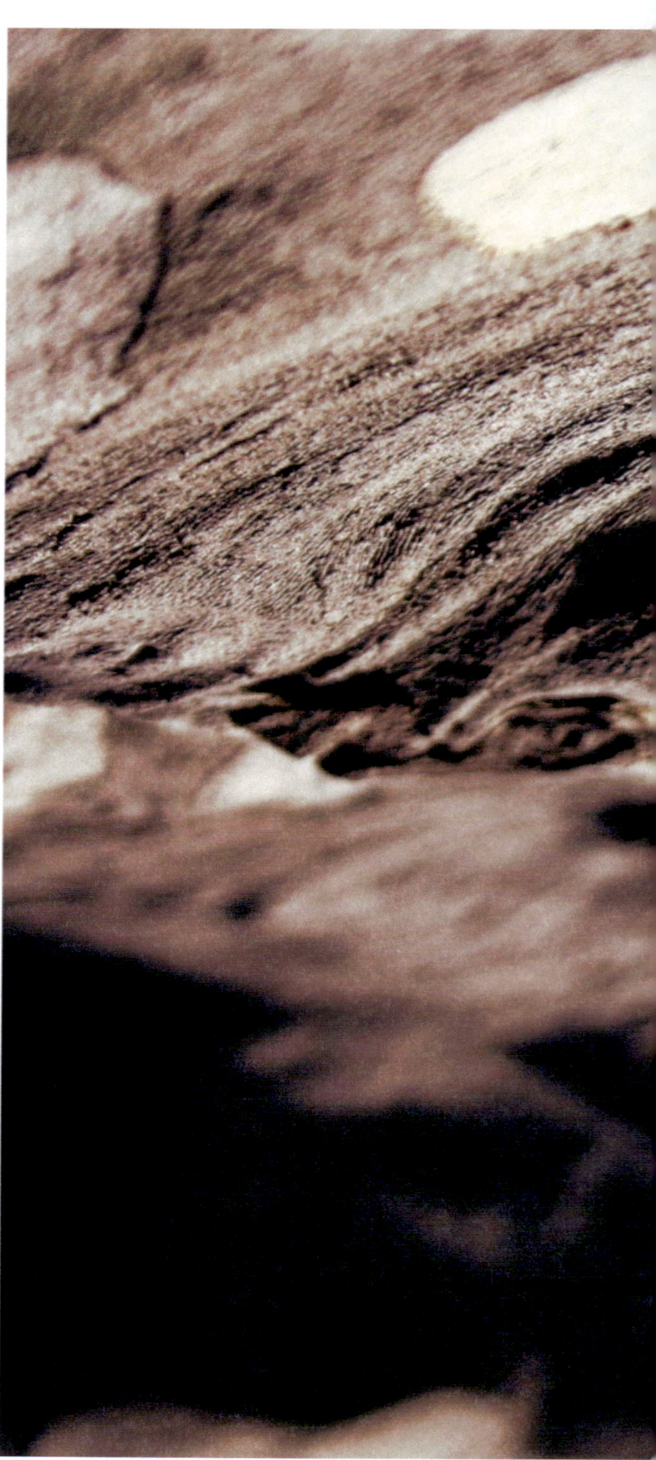

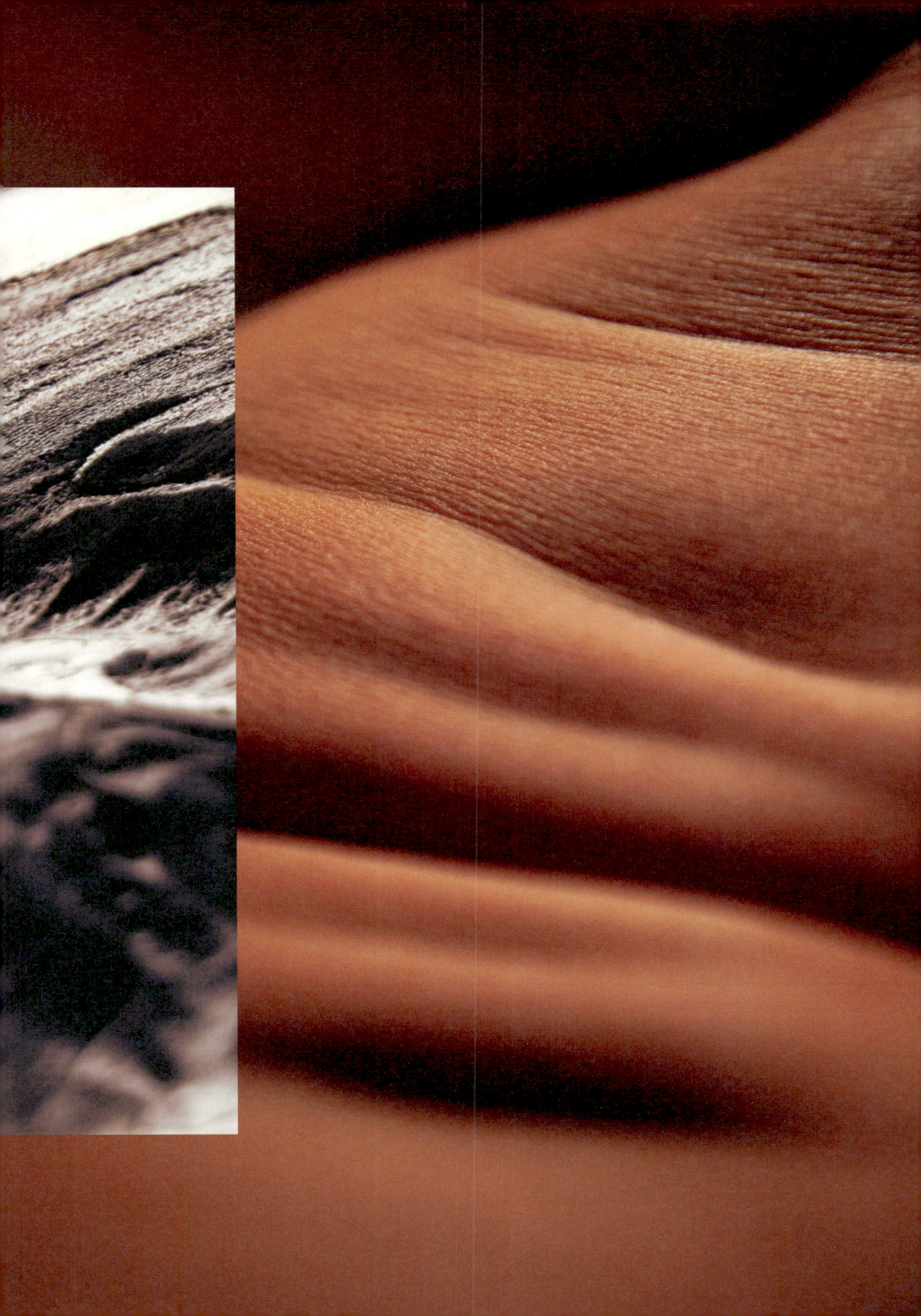

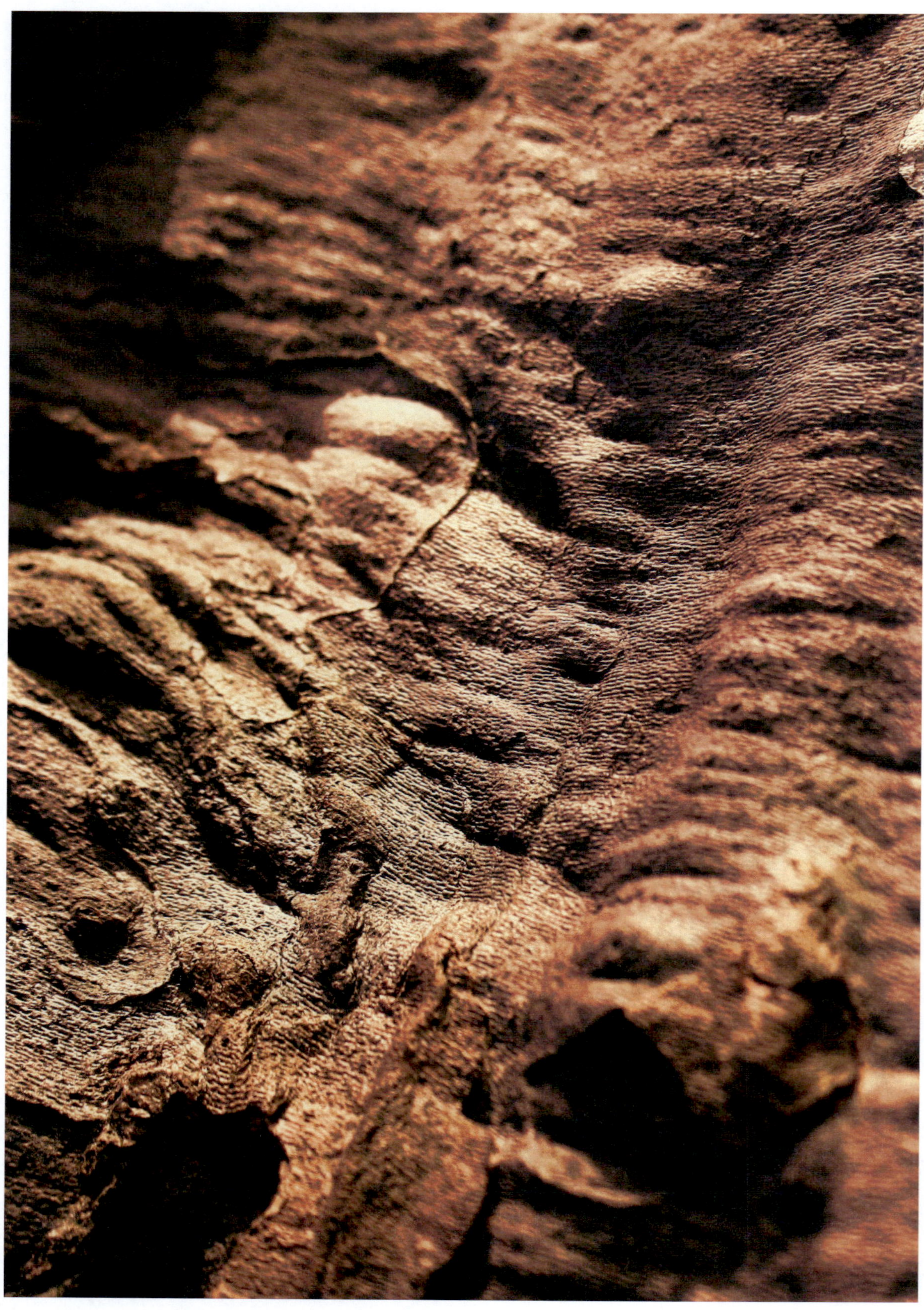

In my distance

In my distance,
I wander through hills
barely held
by the shadow's arms.
I draw circles around them,
show myself exposed
and chase away the wild.
In my distance I discover closeness
and my body its flesh.

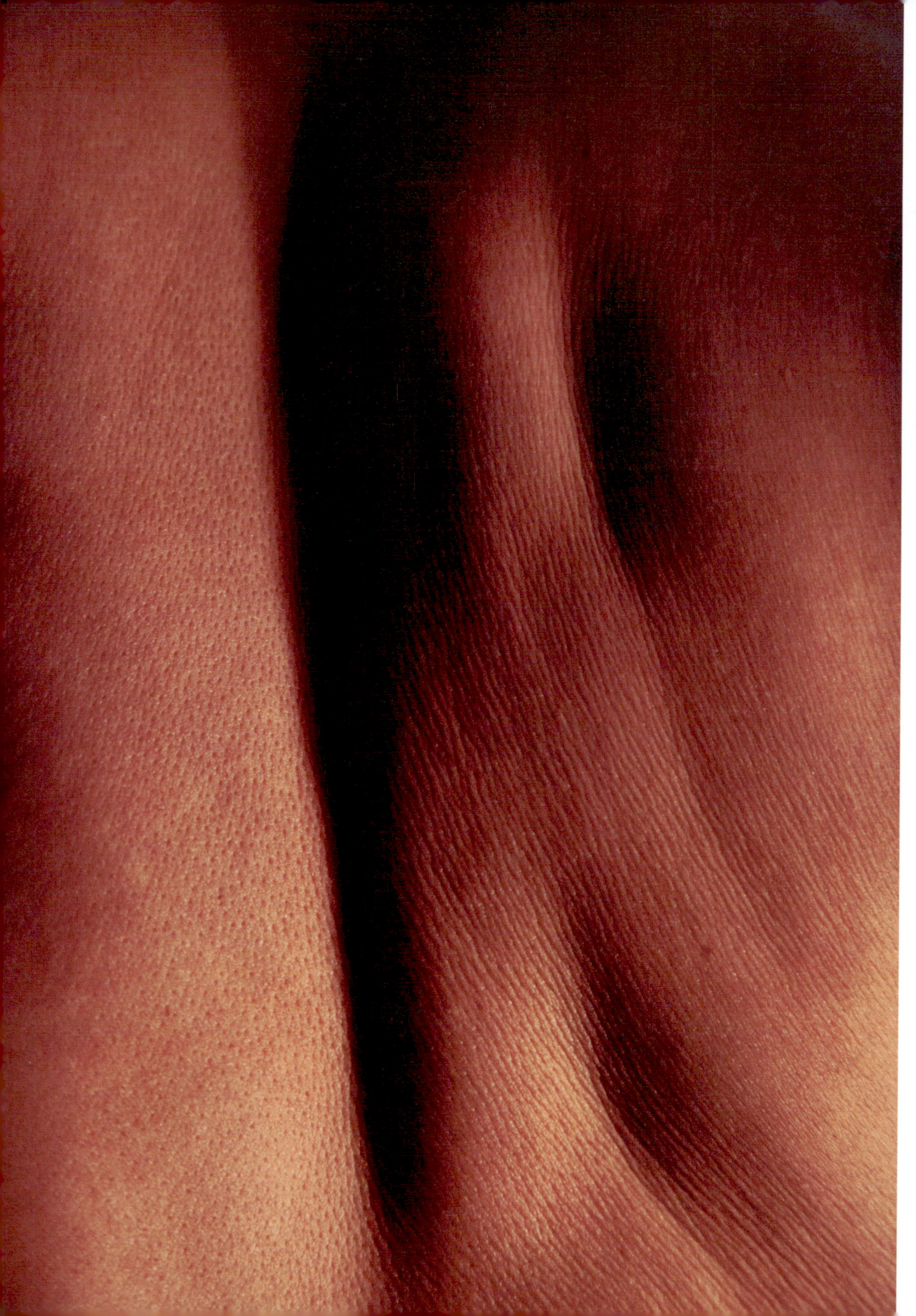

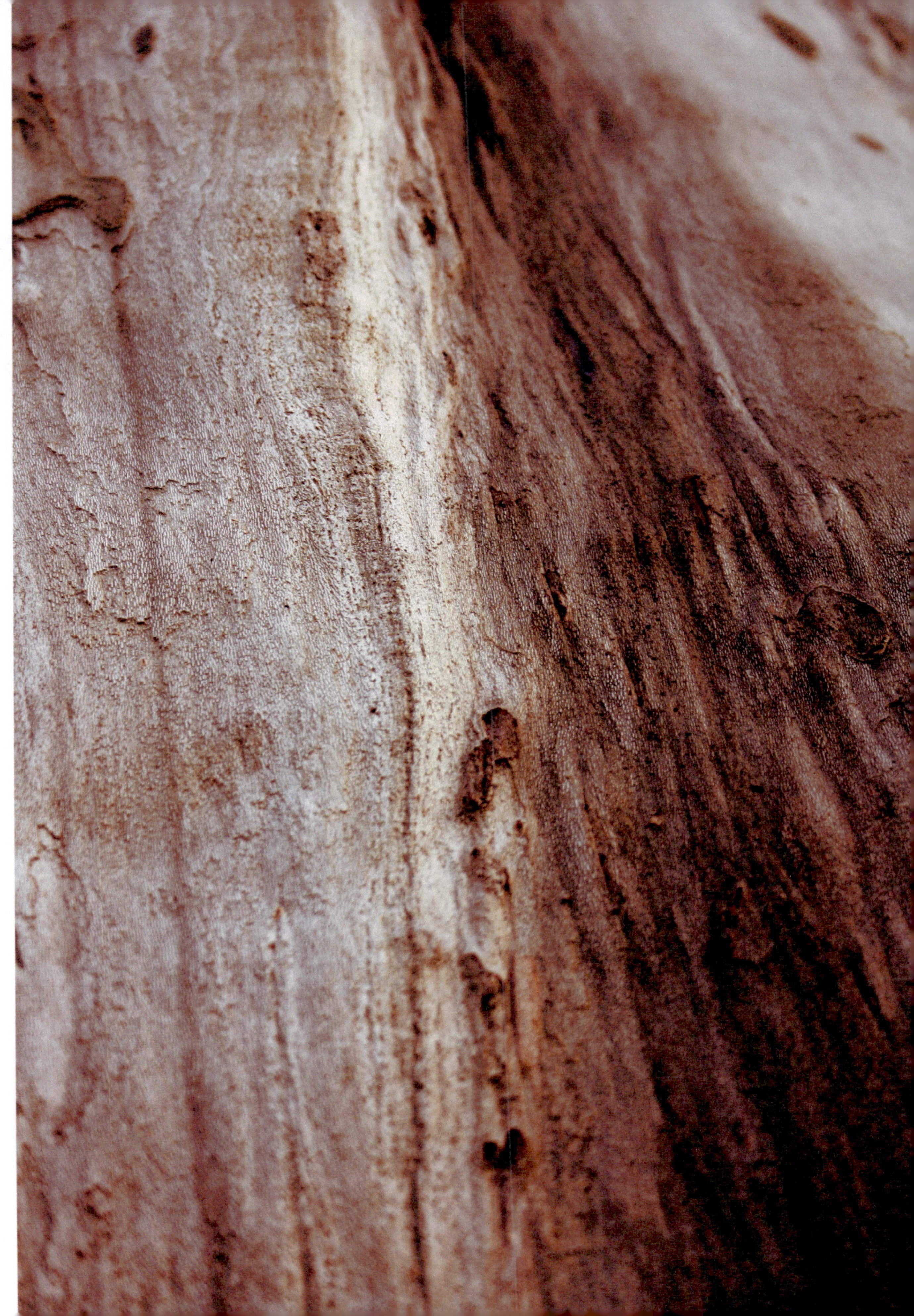

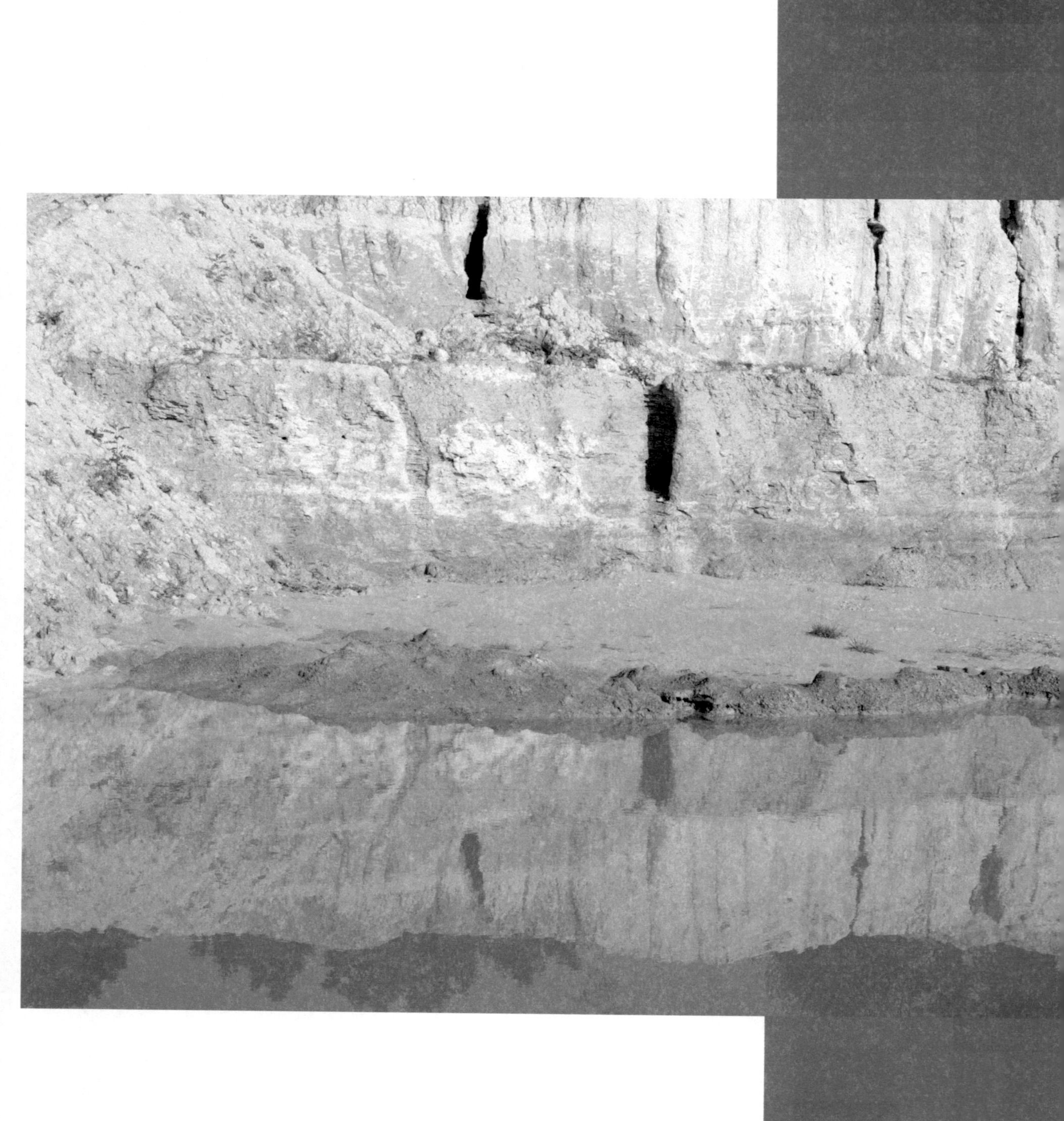

Intermediate space

JACOB BARTMANN

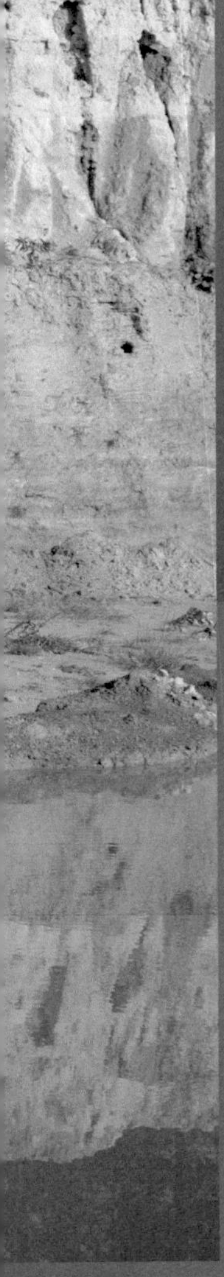

Ich entnahm einer Tongrube Erde und brannte sie Stück für Stück in unterschiedlichen Temperaturstufen. Je nach Brenngrad veränderte sich der Farbverlauf der Tonerde, den ich dokumentierte. Das Grau des Usprungsmaterials verwandelte sich immer mehr zu Farben die an Hauttöne erinnern. Zusammen, mit den einer Mondlandschaft ähnlichen Fotografien der Tongrube, bildete sich ein Kontrast zwischen Nähe und Distanz.

I took earth from a clay pit and fired it piece by piece at different temperature levels. Depending on the degree of firing, the color gradient of the clay changed, which I documented. The gray of the original material changed more and more to colors reminiscent of skin tones. Together with the photographs of the clay pit, which resemble a lunar landscape, a contrast between closeness and distance was formed.

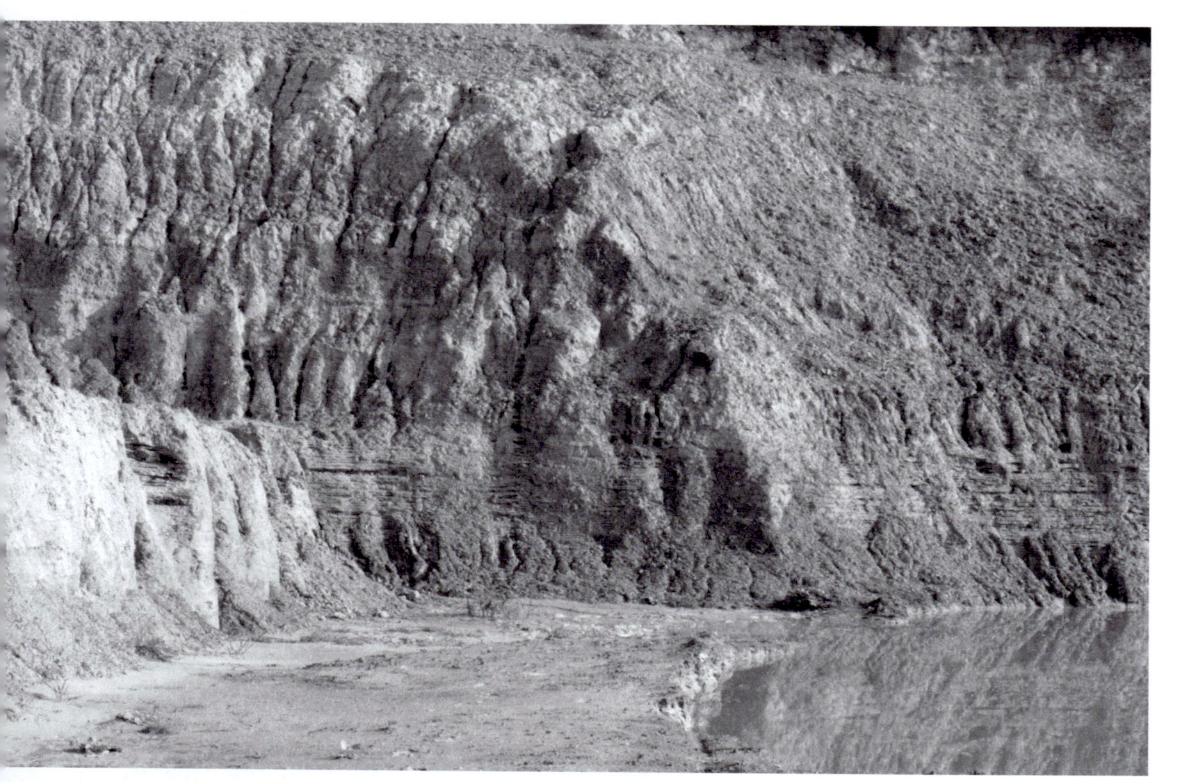

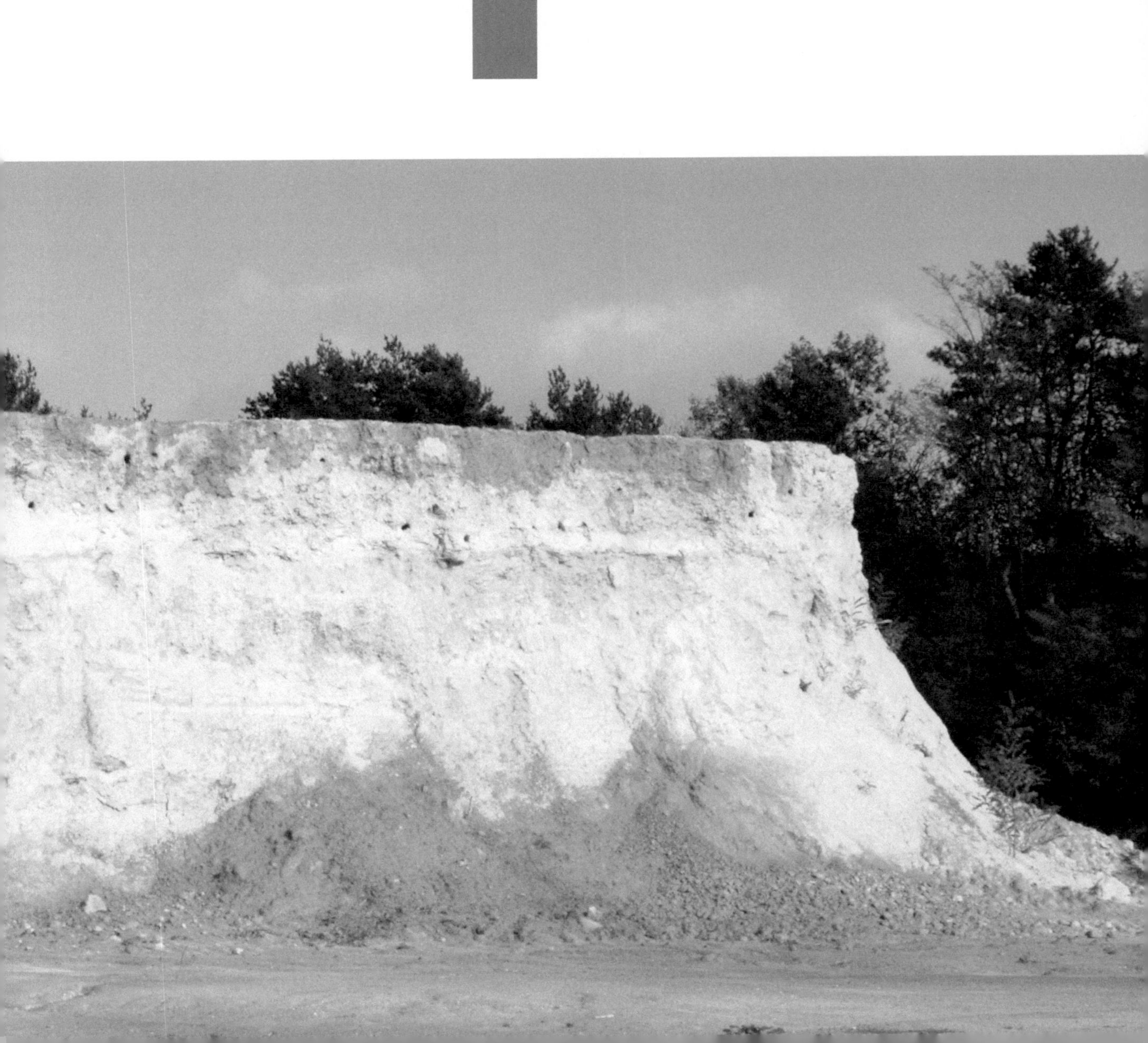

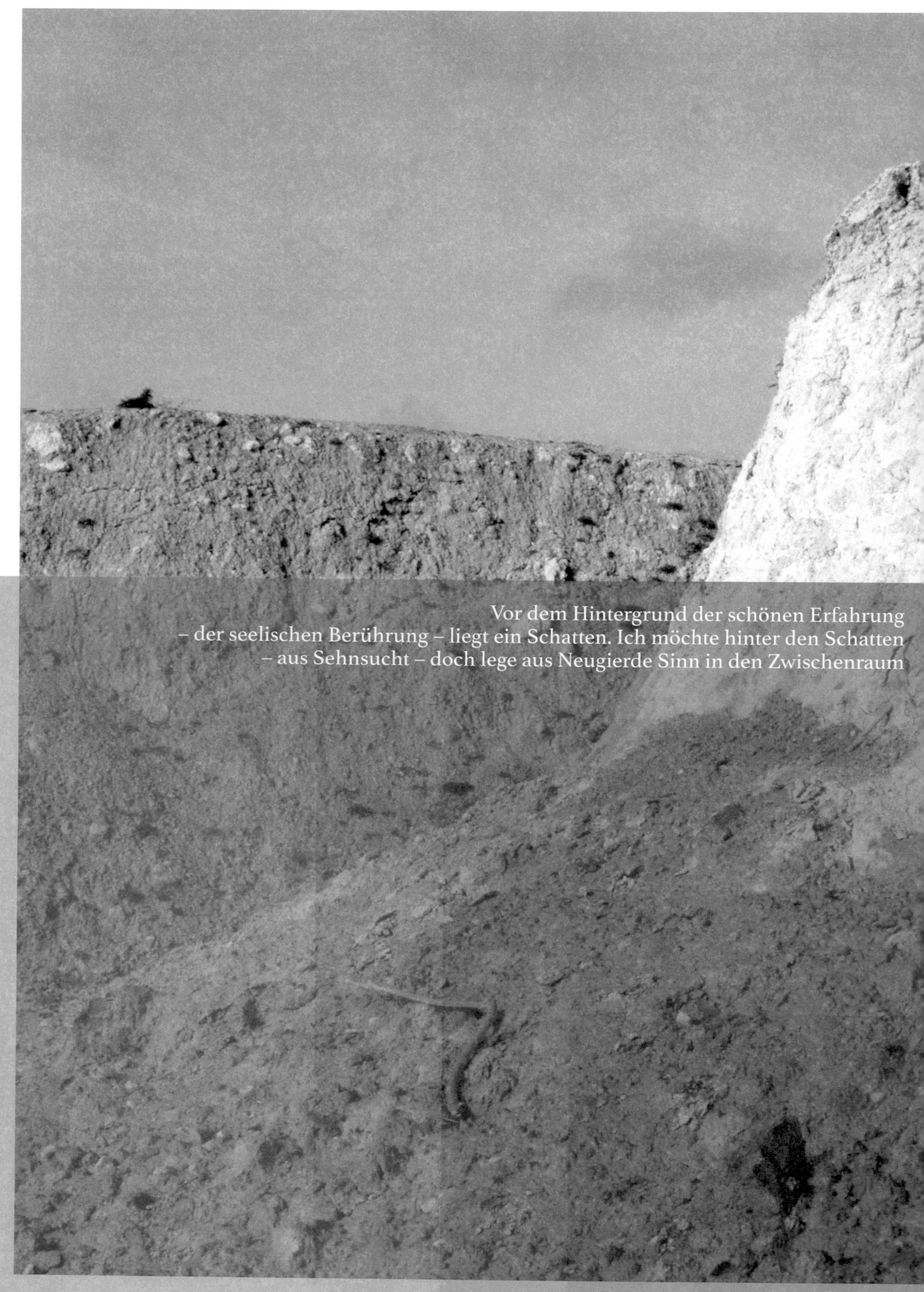

Vor dem Hintergrund der schönen Erfahrung
– der seelischen Berührung – liegt ein Schatten. Ich möchte hinter den Schatten
– aus Sehnsucht – doch lege aus Neugierde Sinn in den Zwischenraum

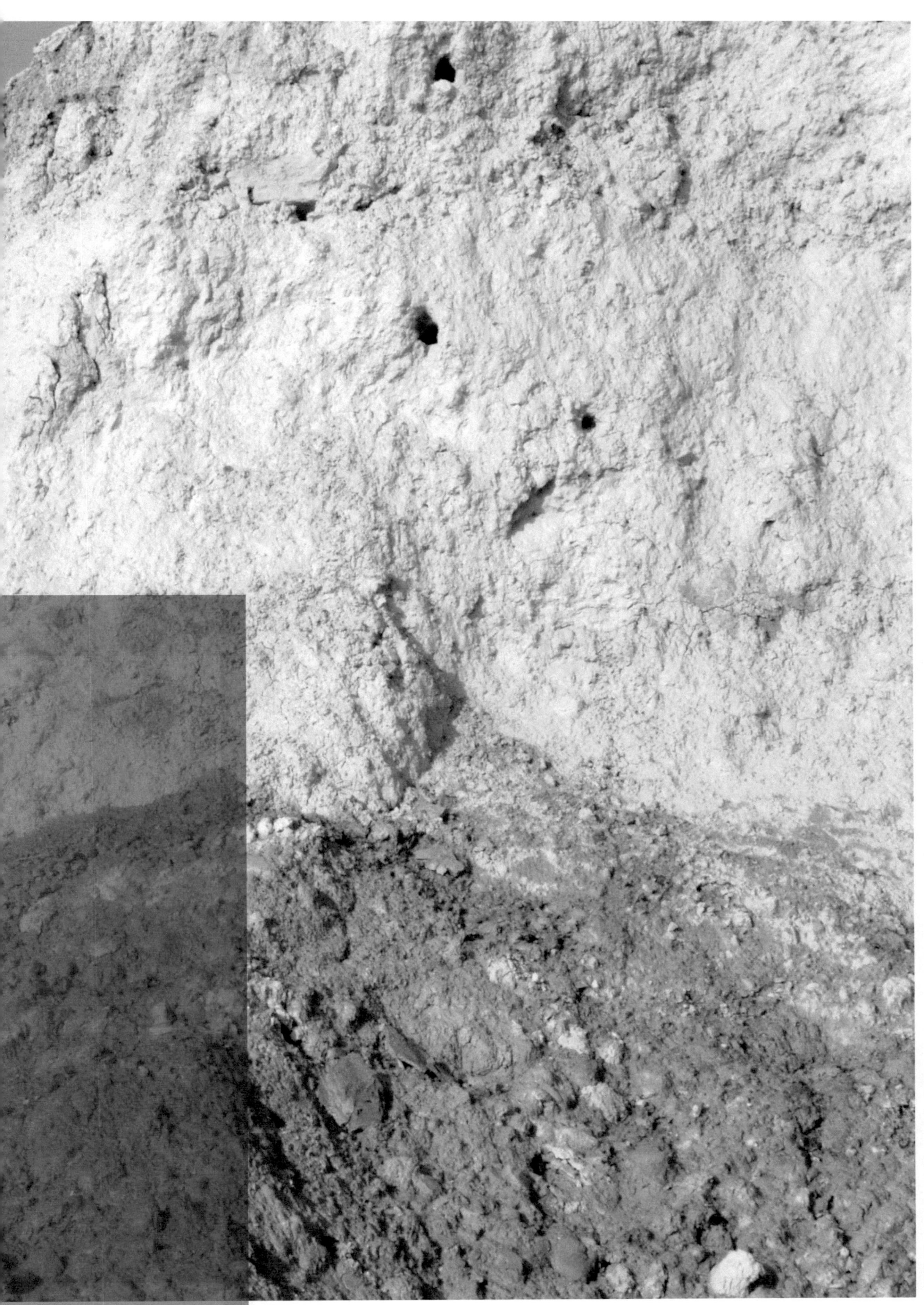

JESSICA KOPPA

Posters Prohibited

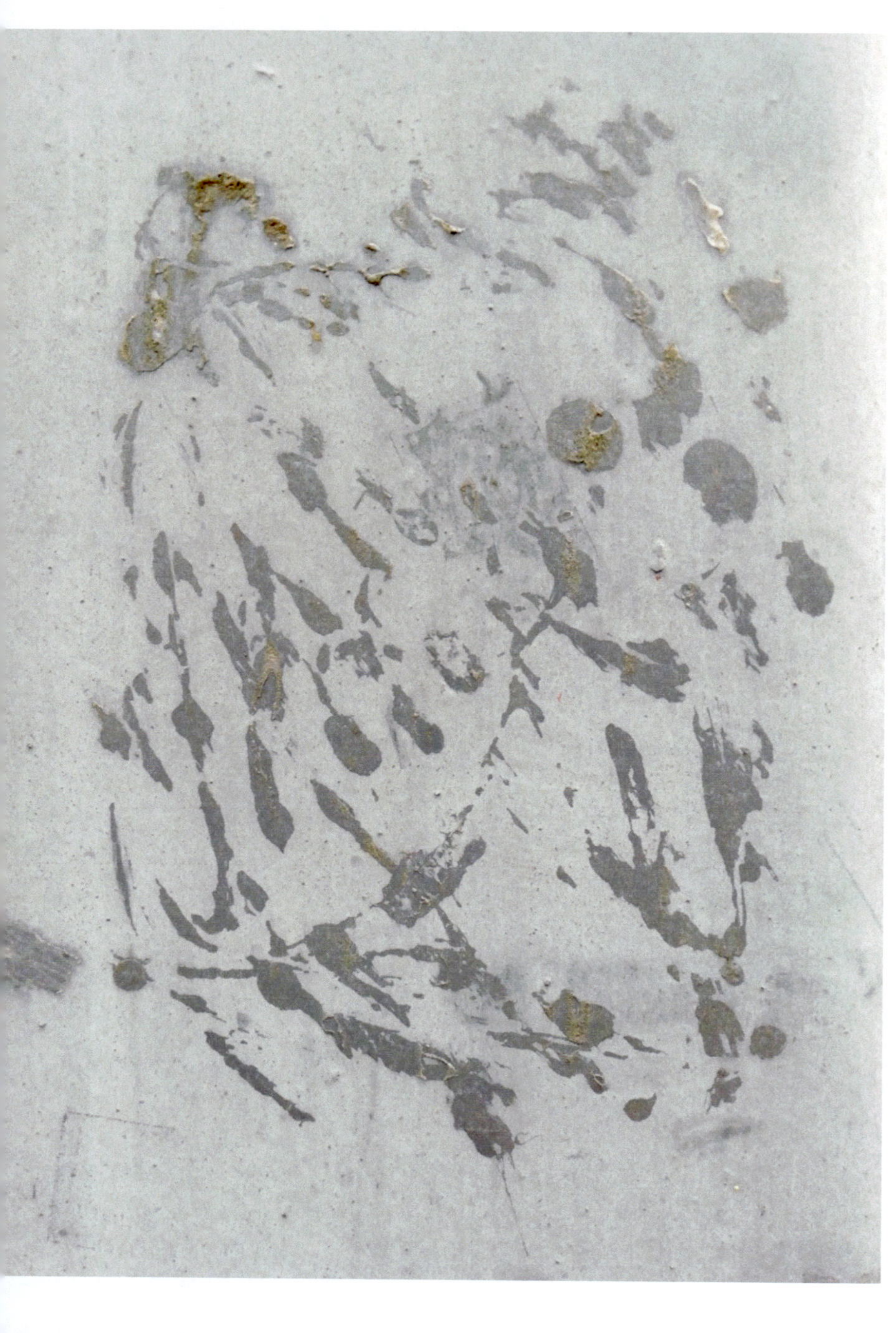

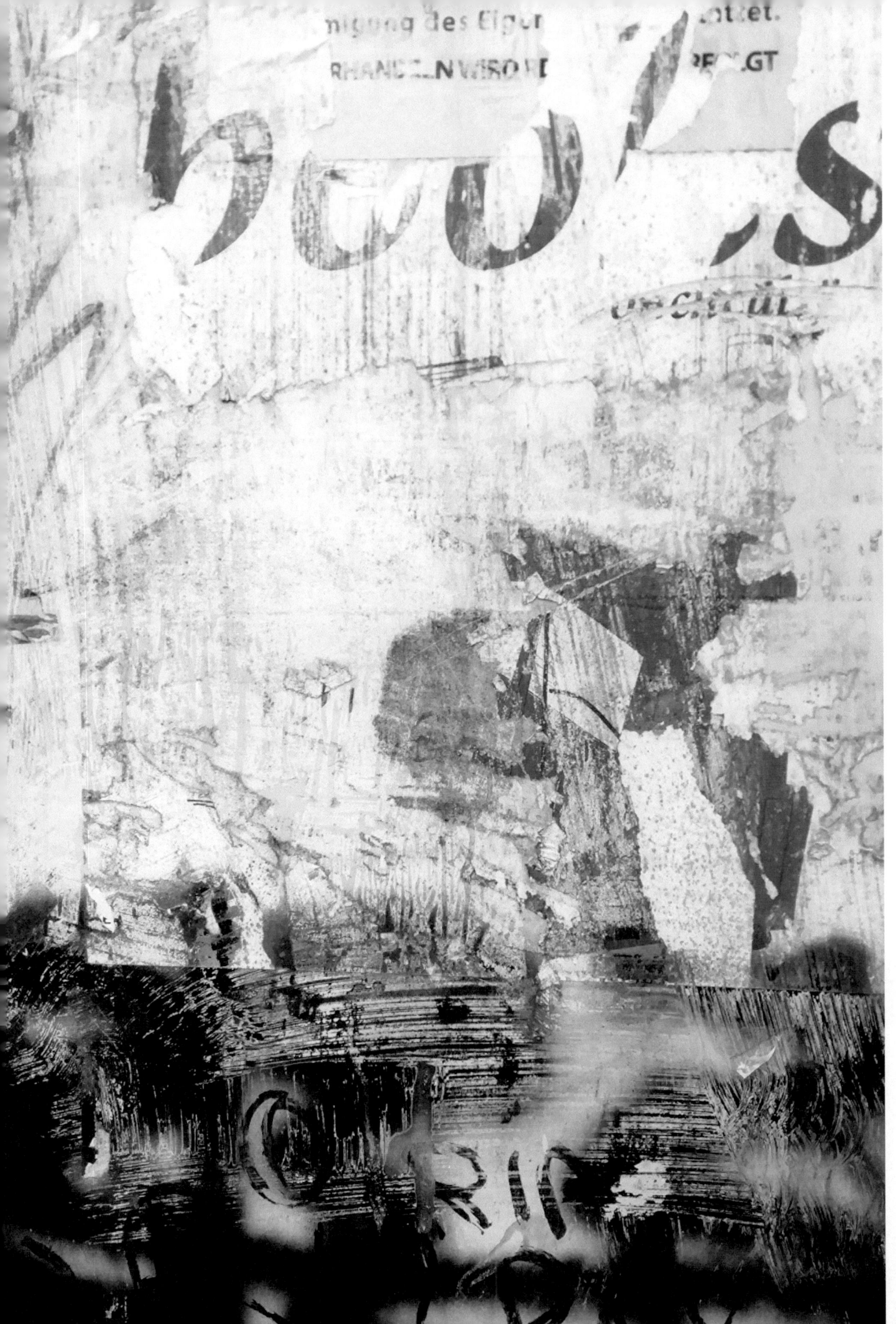

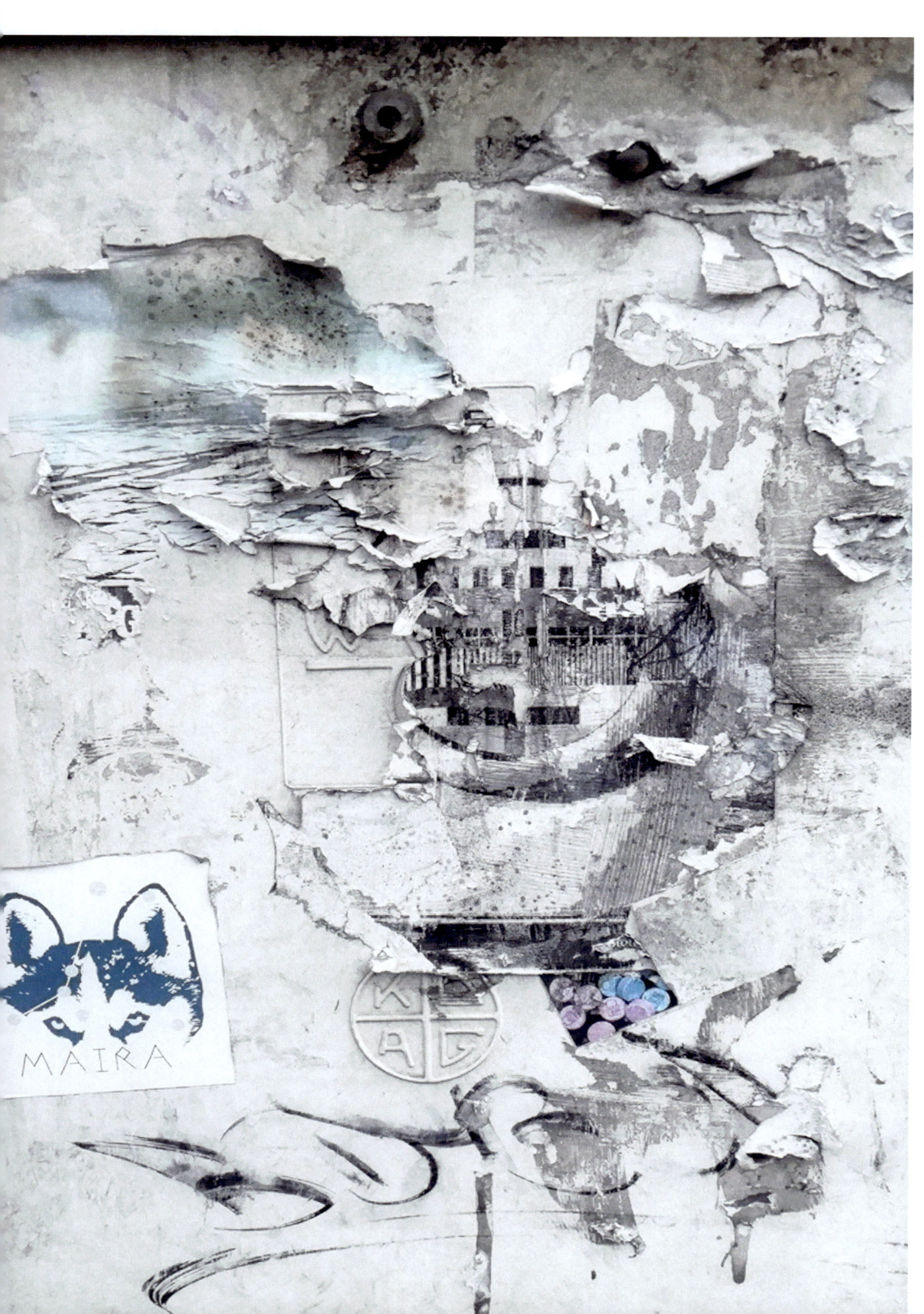

MAIRA

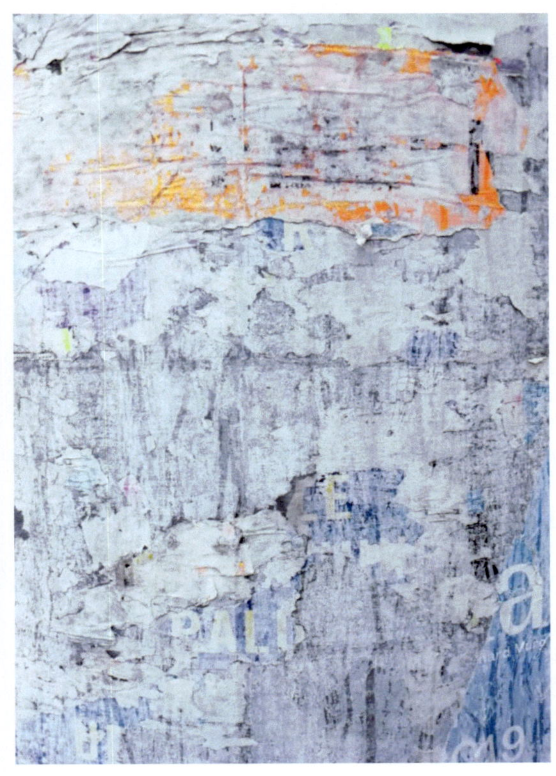

Unauthorized artistic traces in urban settings attract attention. Where is art still possible when museums, galleries, etc. have to remain closed due to the pandemic?

Searching for images, for randomly emerging patterns and forms through the streets, which distract us from the everyday pandemic routine, has drawn my attention to the posters that are obsolete in the current situation.

Nicht genehmigte künstlerische Spuren im urbanen Raum ziehen die Blicke auf sich. Wo ist Kunst noch möglich, wenn aufgrund der Maßnahmen der Pandemie kulturelle Orte geschlossen bleiben müssen?

Die Suche nach Bildern, nach sich zufällig ergebenden Mustern und Formen, die vom alltäglichen, pandemischen Trott durch die Straßen ablenken, hat meinen Blick auf die in der jetzigen Situation obsoleten Plakate gelenkt.

Der Gedanke, künstlerische Gestal-
tungsmöglichkeiten innerhalb der Straßen einer Stadt anzusiedeln und Kunst
in den öffentlichen Raum zu platzieren
kommt auf.

Plakate und Sticker, die wie Collagen
übereinandergeschichtet sind, deuten
neue Bildwelten an, die abseits von
Kommerz, Institutionen und dem
Monopol von Plakatierfirmen einen
eigenen Ausdruck finden können.

Sie scheinen nur für sich zu stehen;
zeigen das Zufällige sowie das
Abwesende und können identitäts-
stiftendes Phänomen sein, um die
städtische Anonymität durch Spuren
der Aneignung zu kompensieren.

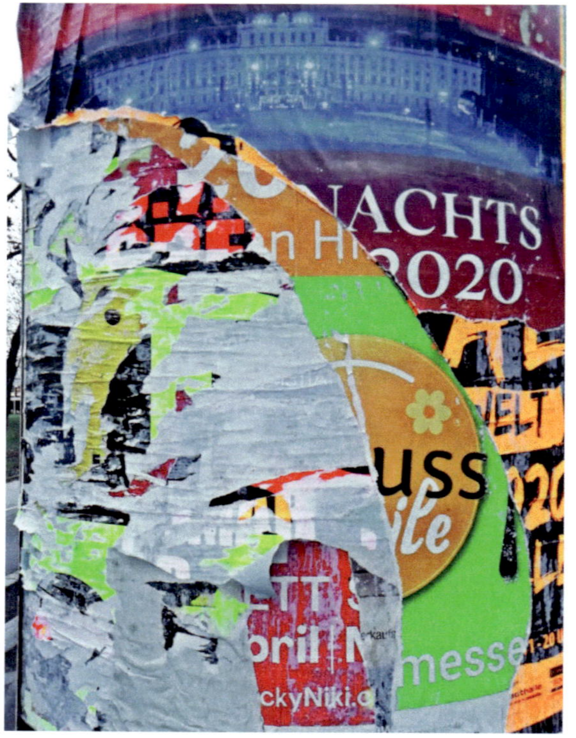

The idea of locating artistic creations within the streets of a city and placing art in
public spaces comes to mind.
Posters and stickers, layered on top of
each other like collages, open a new
world of possibilities for the visual arts,
one where artists can express
themselves independently away from
commercialism, institutions and the
monopoly of poster companies.

No bill-sticking. They seem to be
there only for themselves, showing
the random as well as the absent
while creating an identity, to
compensate urban anonymity
by signs of appropriation.

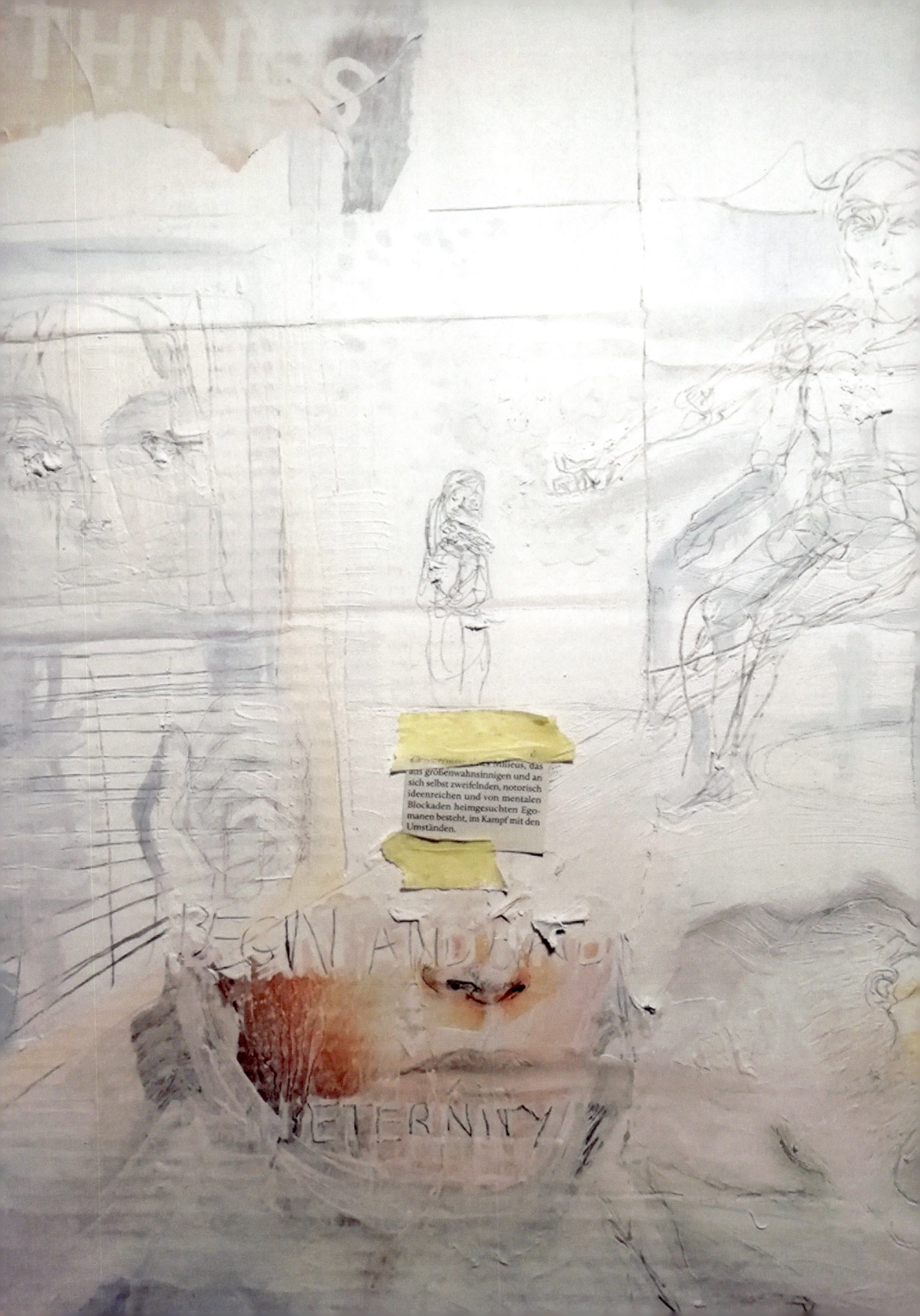

THIN
das
aus größenwahnsinnigen und an
sich selbst zweifelnden, notorisch
ideenreichen und von mentalen
Blockaden heimgesuchten Ego-
manen besteht, im Kampf mit den
Umständen.
BEGIN AND END
ETERNITY

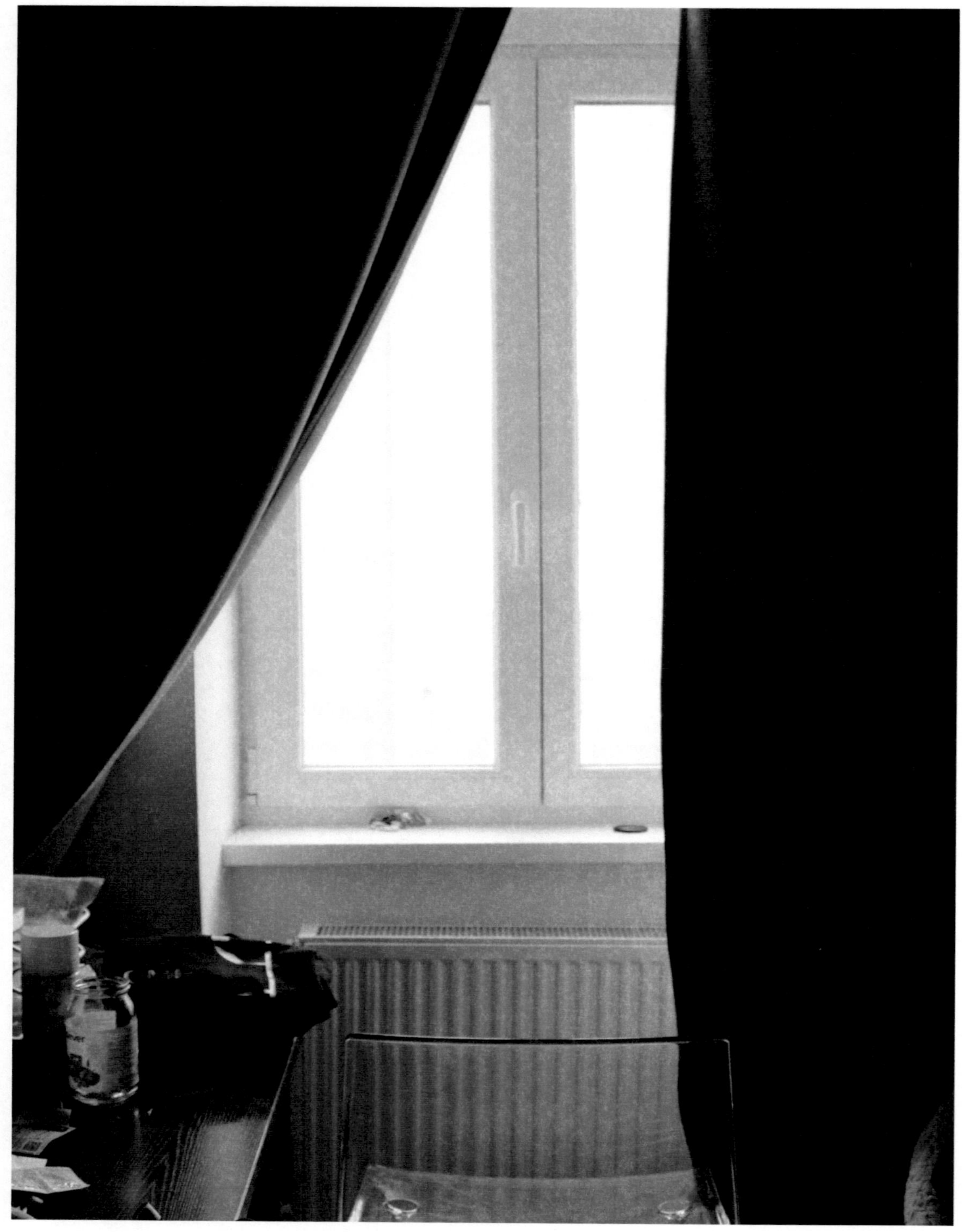

Zuhause sein

SVENJA ZEWE

Zuhause sein
Ein neuer Ort
Ein neuer Raum
Ein Versuch

Geborgenheit

Be at home
A new place
A new room
One try

Security

Gegenstände, Rituale und Gerüche
Das weiche Kissen spüren
Wenn der Kopf schwer wird
Sich fallen lassen
Noch einmal den Geruch einatmen
Und dann ausatmen

Objects, rituals, and smells
Feel the soft pillow
When your head gets heavy
To let yourself fall
Inhale the smell again
And then breathe out

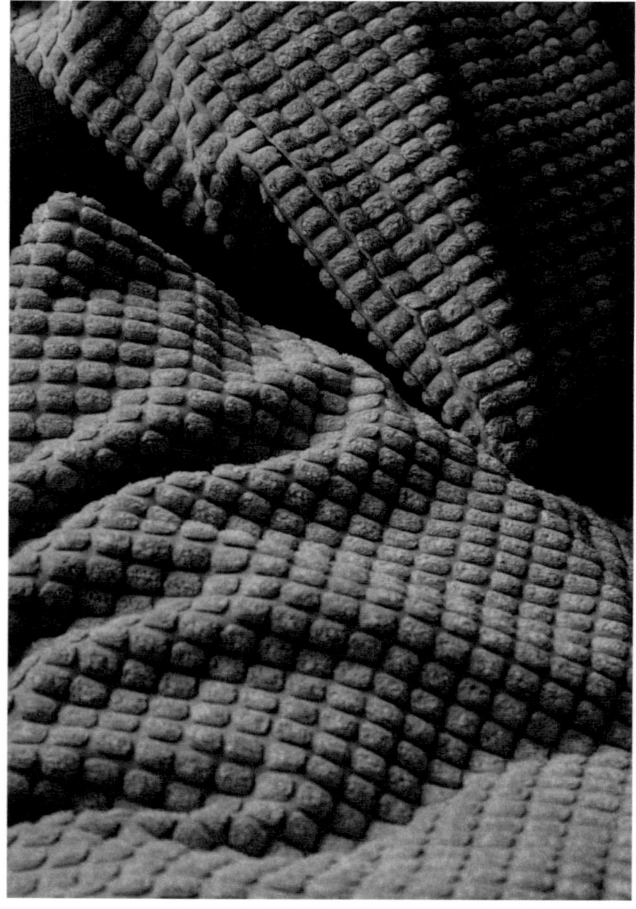

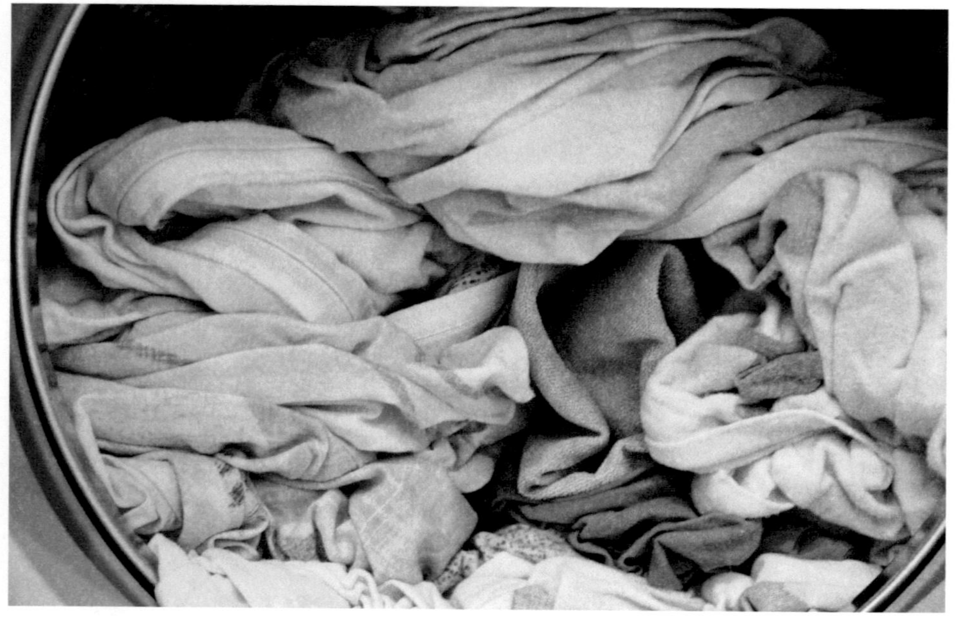

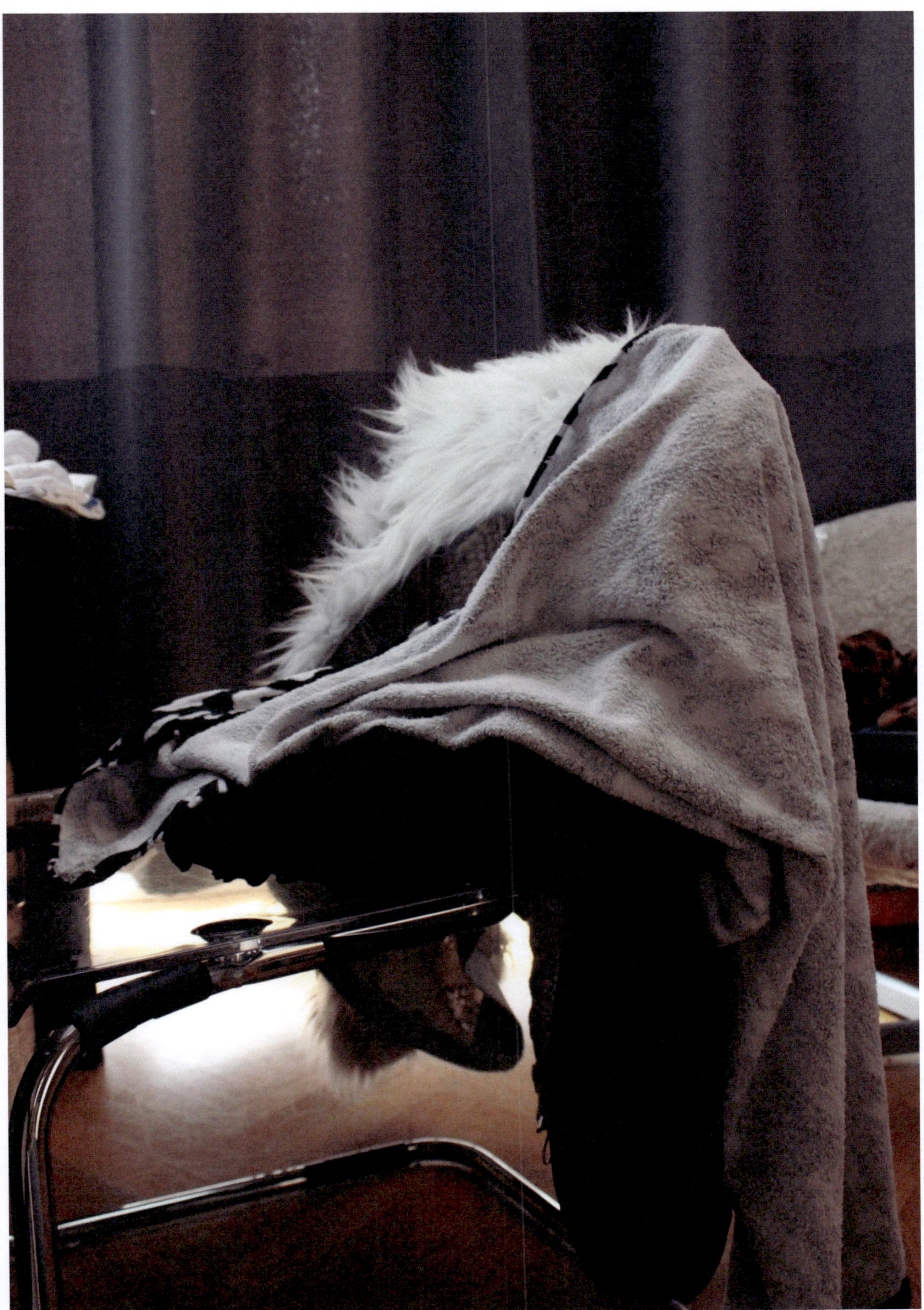

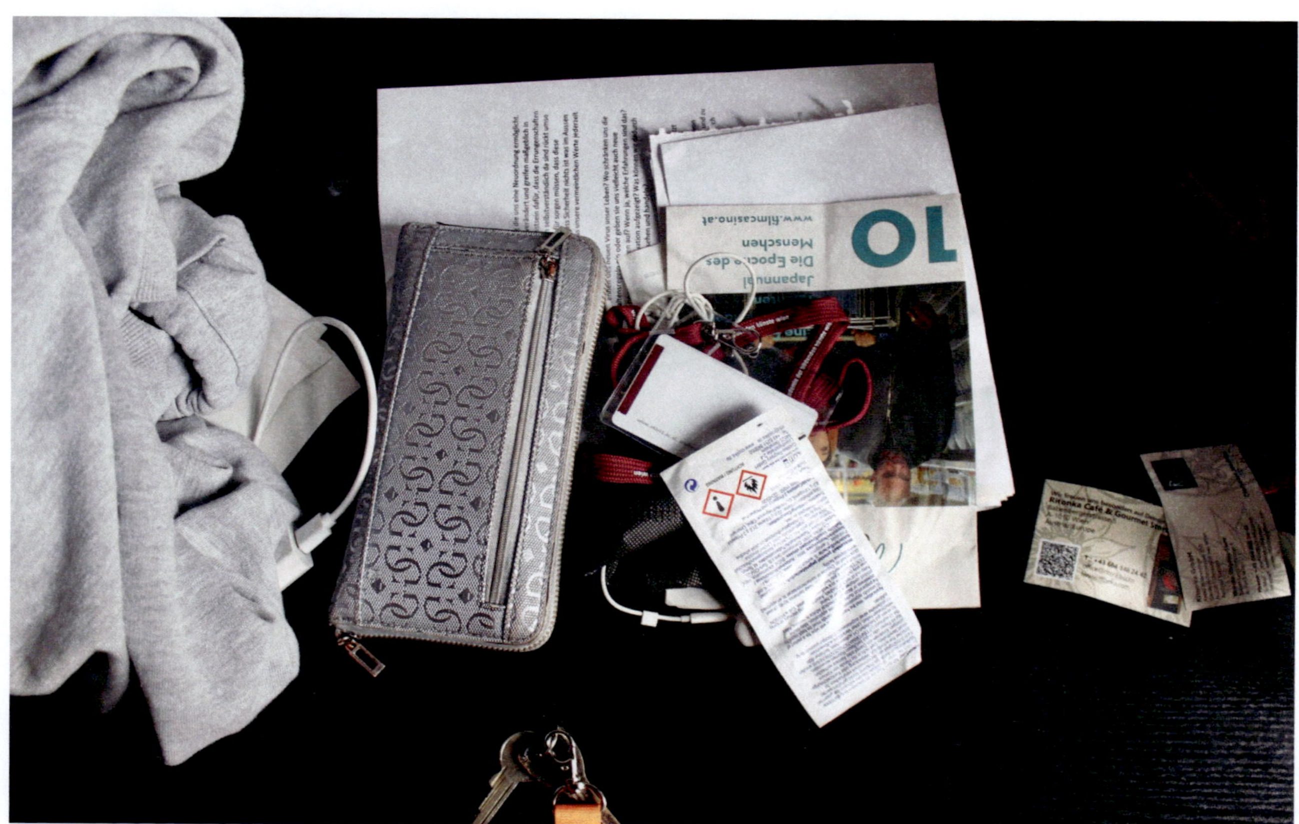

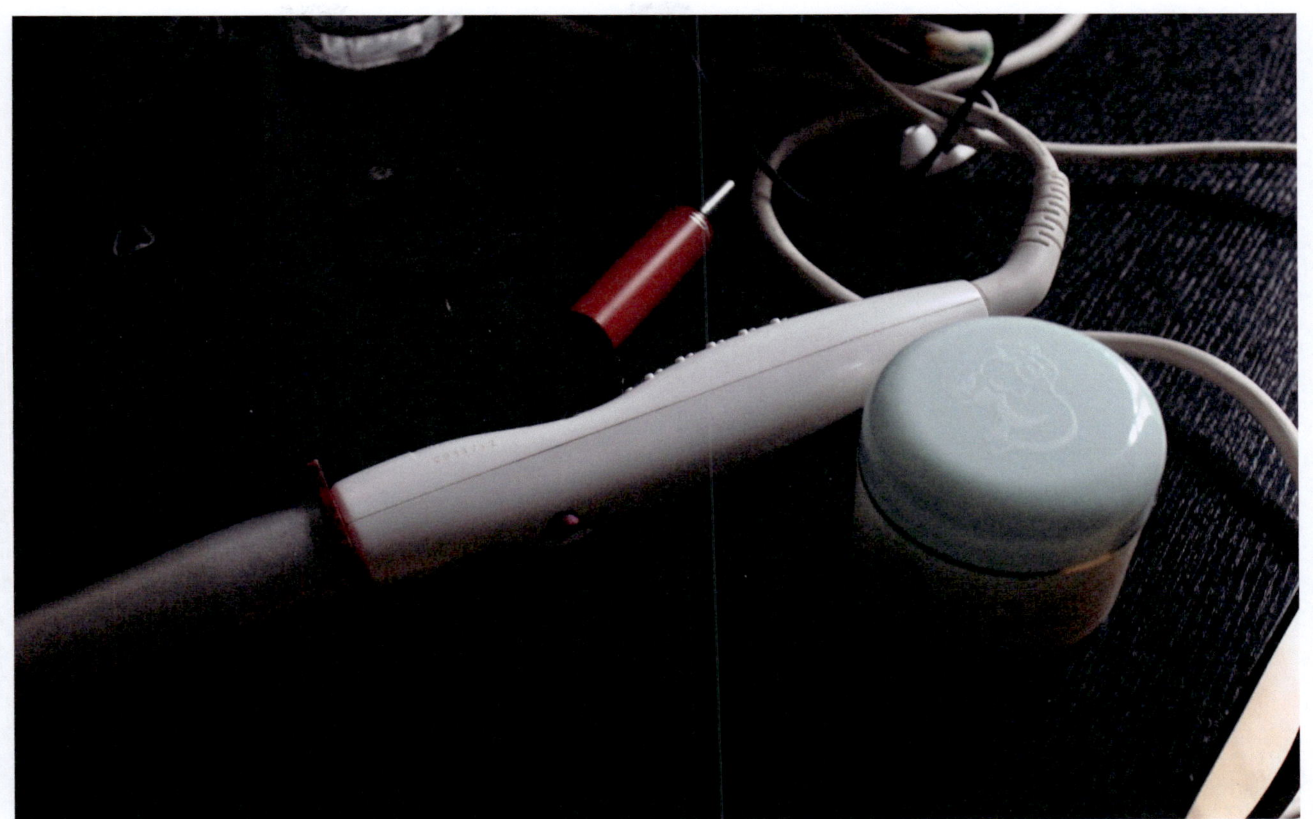

Der Koffer bleibt versteckt.
Er steht ganz still hinter dem Vorhang.
Ein Koffer wird nur gepackt,
wenn man bereit ist zu gehen.
Aber das bin ich nicht, also bleibt er
dort wo er ist
ganz still hinter dem Vorhang

Silber darf es sein.

Spüren, wie das Innenfutter langsam abfällt.
Die Ärmel riechen leicht nach Zigaretten.
In den Taschen sind einige Tabakreste.

Es ist schön,
ich kenne sie,
so als ob wir Freunde wären.

The suitcase remains hidden.
It stands very still behind the curtain.
A suitcase is only packed
when you're ready to go.
But I'm not, so he stays
where he is
very quiet behind the curtain

It can be silver.

To feel how the inner lining slowly falls off.
The sleeves smell slightly of cigarettes.
There are some tobacco remains in the
pockets.

It is nice,
I know you,
like we're friends

Times of change bring about the
possibility of a dialogue with oneself.
Reflection of the present state, throwing
oneself into perspective, on the ground,
dancing wild, or breathing in front
of a mirror.

This is an experiment; a visual
exploration of the intimate, raw,
and often unpleasant confrontation
of a human with herself.
The body, the mind, torn apart, and
yet inseparable. Eyes turned inward,
outward. The burden of living, the
tingling of breath, considering oneself
as a surface, then fading back into
one's head completely. There could
be peace and calmness, in being still,
if one endures it even within our
pulsating world of repeated movement.

Closing borders inward and outward,
mourning empty cafés and houses,
then silence. Craving a conversation
with random strangers. Sharing
breakfast with friends. An attempt of
sweeping the heaviness away, lying.

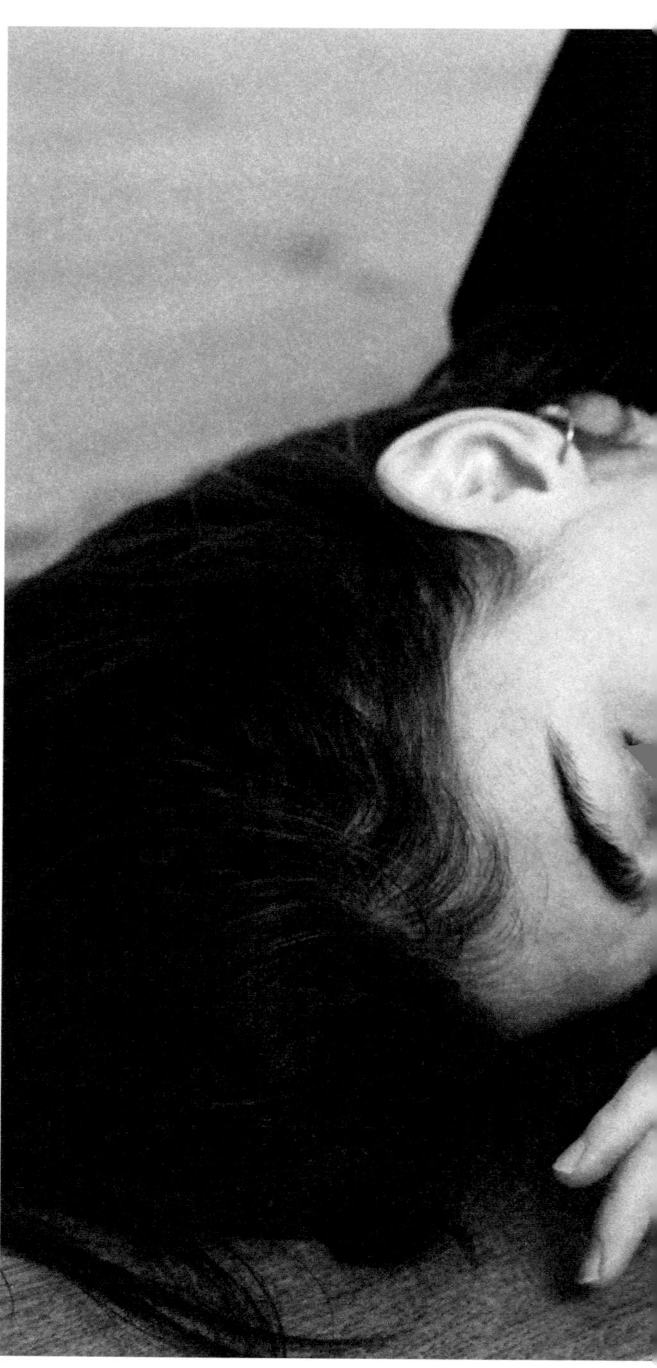

Fragments of Being

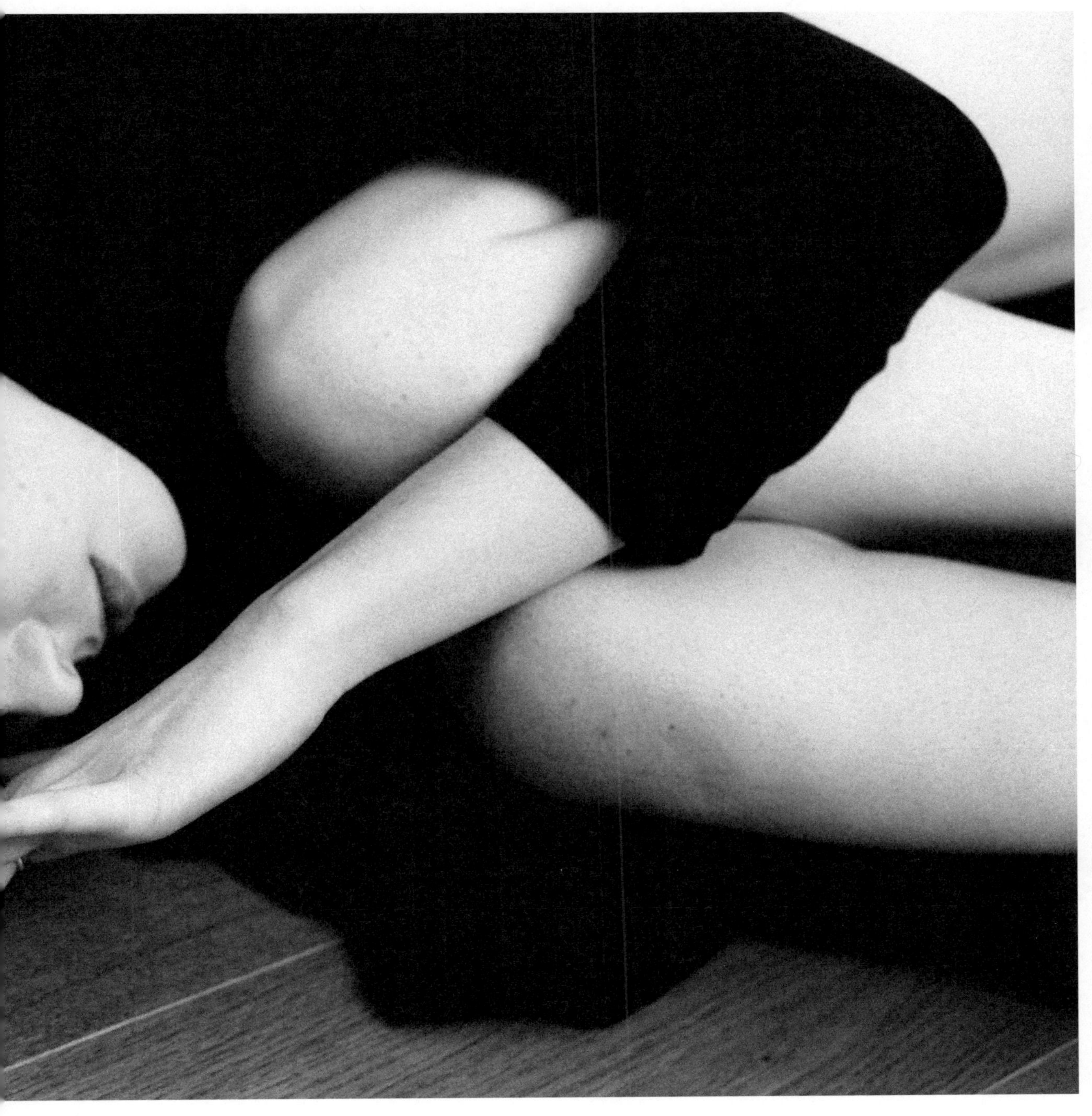

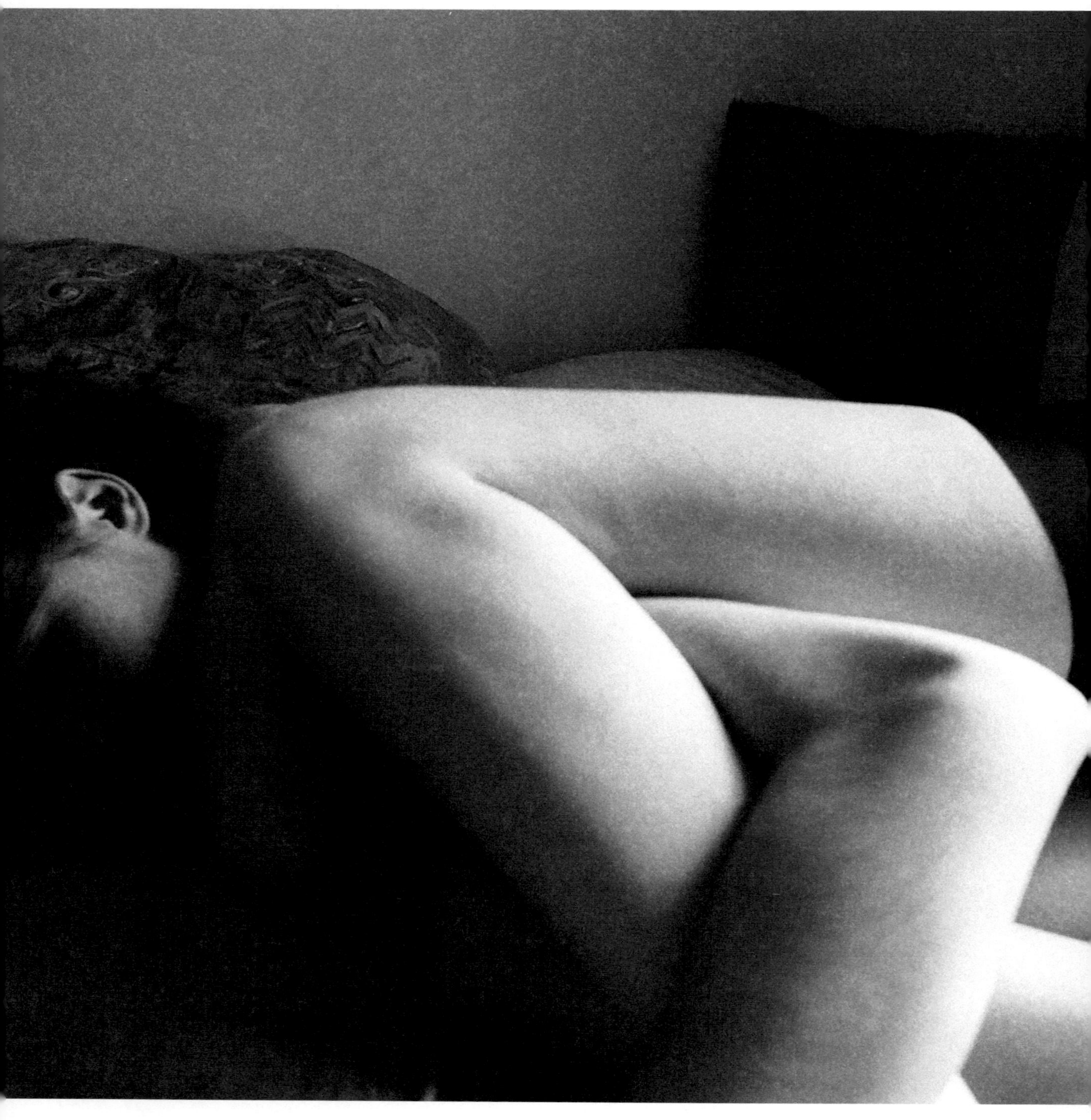

I am trapped in a perpetual state
of breaking.
My body suspended in the act
of implosion.
Forces infinitely pulling inward to no avail.
Life teeming on the surface.
In the middle, a dead center. A vacuum.
In it, a question.
I am trapped in a perpetual state
of fragmentation.
I am being dismembered.
My toes. My feet. My legs.
My fingers. My hands. My arms.
Torn off. Removed.
My hips. My head. Taken away.
Donated, gifted, sold.
My consciousness remains in my torso.
My chest.
Empty space. A vacuum. In it, silence.
I am trapped in a perpetual state of...

Susi Heger

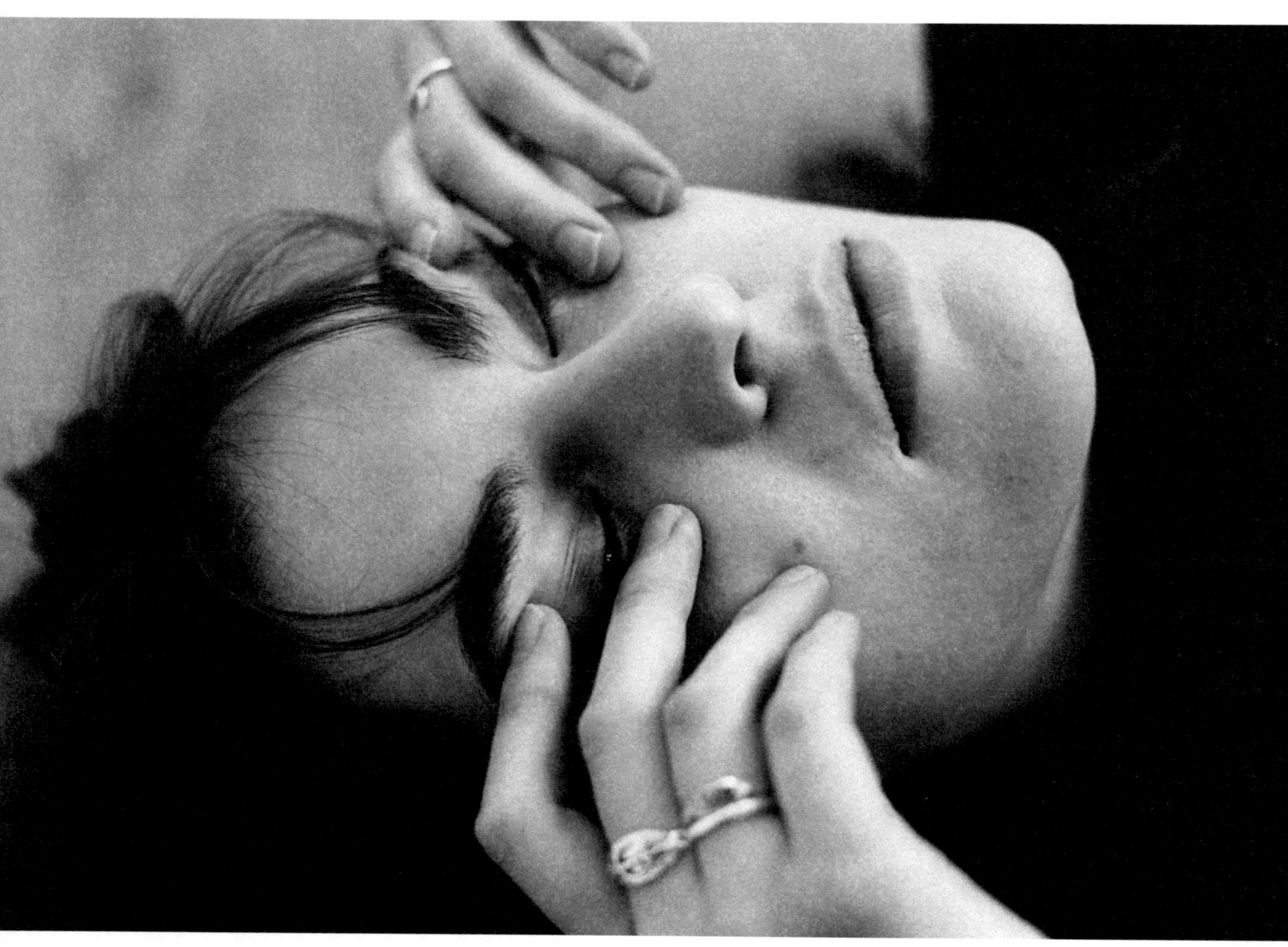

Zeiten der Veränderung schaffen eine
Möglichkeit zum Dialog mit sich selbst. Nach-
denken über den Momentanzustand, sich
selbst in andere Perspektiven setzen,
am Boden, beim Tanzen, oder vor dem
Spiegel, wo man sich selbst ins Gesicht starrt.

Ein Experiment, Abbild einer ehrlichen Kon-
frontation mit dem Selbst. Körper und Gedan-
ken werden getrennt, um sich später wieder
zusammenzufügen. Augen nach
innen, dann nach außen gerichtet. Die
Alltagslast spüren, den ruhigen Atem, sich als
pure Oberfläche betrachten,

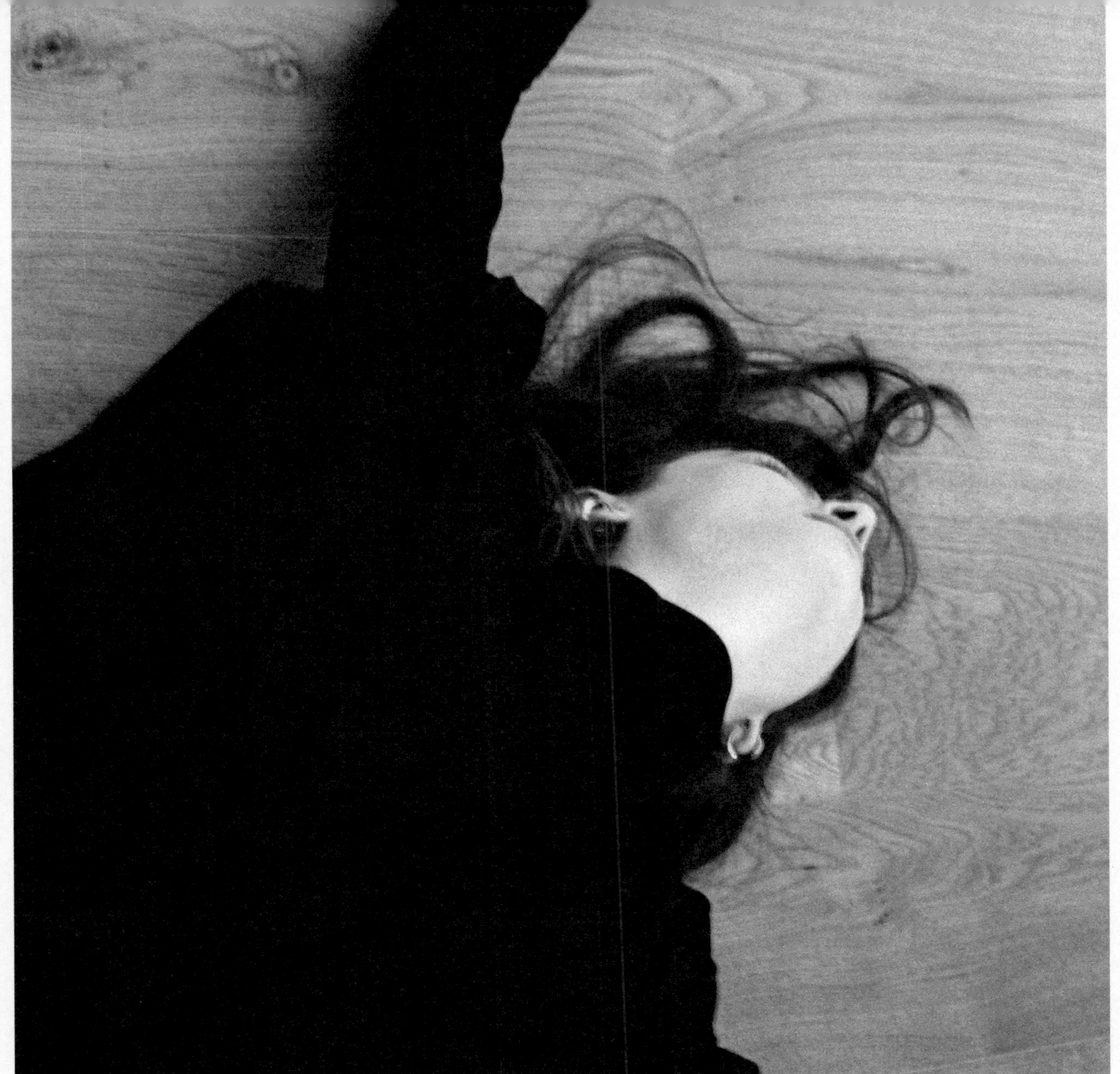

um anschließend zurück in seinen
eigenen Geist zu finden.

Eine Art Zufriedenheit liegt in der Stille,
auch wenn diese oft nicht leicht zu finden ist.

Grenzen werden geschlossen – nach innen
und außen – wir trauern verlassenen Cafés
und Orten nach. Dann der Stille. Wir sehnen
uns nach Gesprächen mit einsamen
Fremden der Straße. Sehnen uns das
Frühstücksmenü mit Freunden zu teilen.
Selbst in der Stille kehrt sich mitunter
die Leichtigkeit von uns ab.

ELKE LEITHNER

Einblicke

„Meine Gewohnheit ins
Kaffeehaus zu gehen um
dort Freunde zu treffen,
den besten Kuchen der
Welt zu essen, Menschen
zu beobachten, sie zu
zeichnen oder einfach
Zeitung zu lesen, mich kurz
aufzuwärmen, auszuruhen,
leer zu werden…

…alles das geht momentan
nicht. Ich kann diese
Aufladeorte nur von
außen beobachten,
muss neue Wege,
neue Räume finden.
Sehe nur die Spiegelung…
den abwesenden
Raum…“

"My habit of going to
the coffee house to
meet friends, eating
the best cake in the world,
watch people, draw them
or just to read the
newspaper, to warm
up for a moment,
rest, empty my mind…

…all that is not possible
at the moment. I can only
find these recharging
places from the outside,
have to find new ways,
new spaces.
I only see the reflection…
the absent space…"

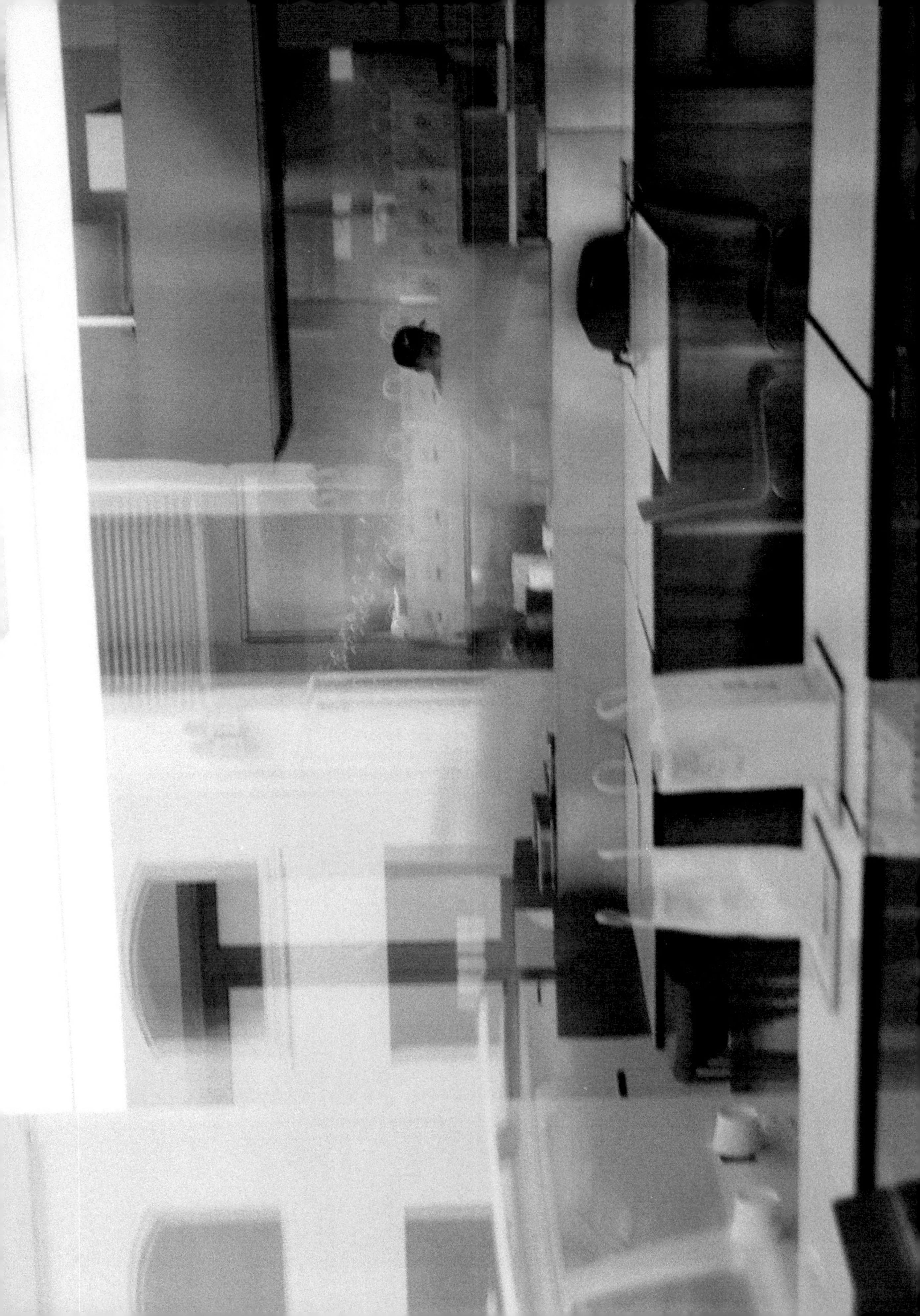

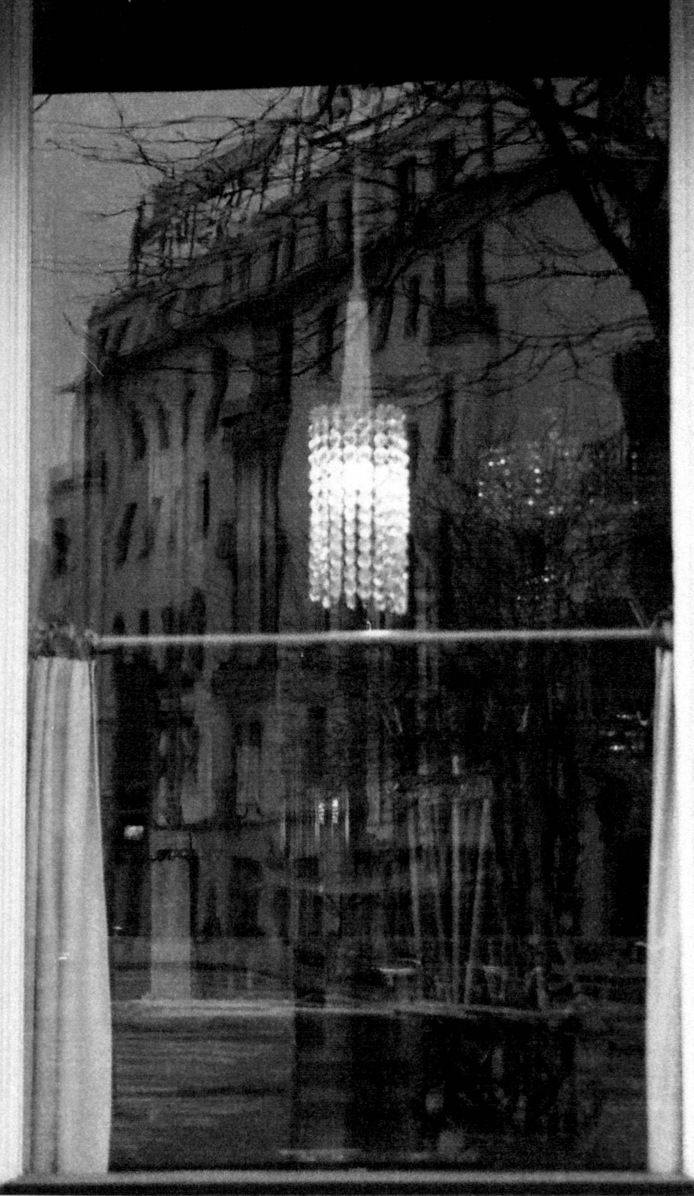

CAFE

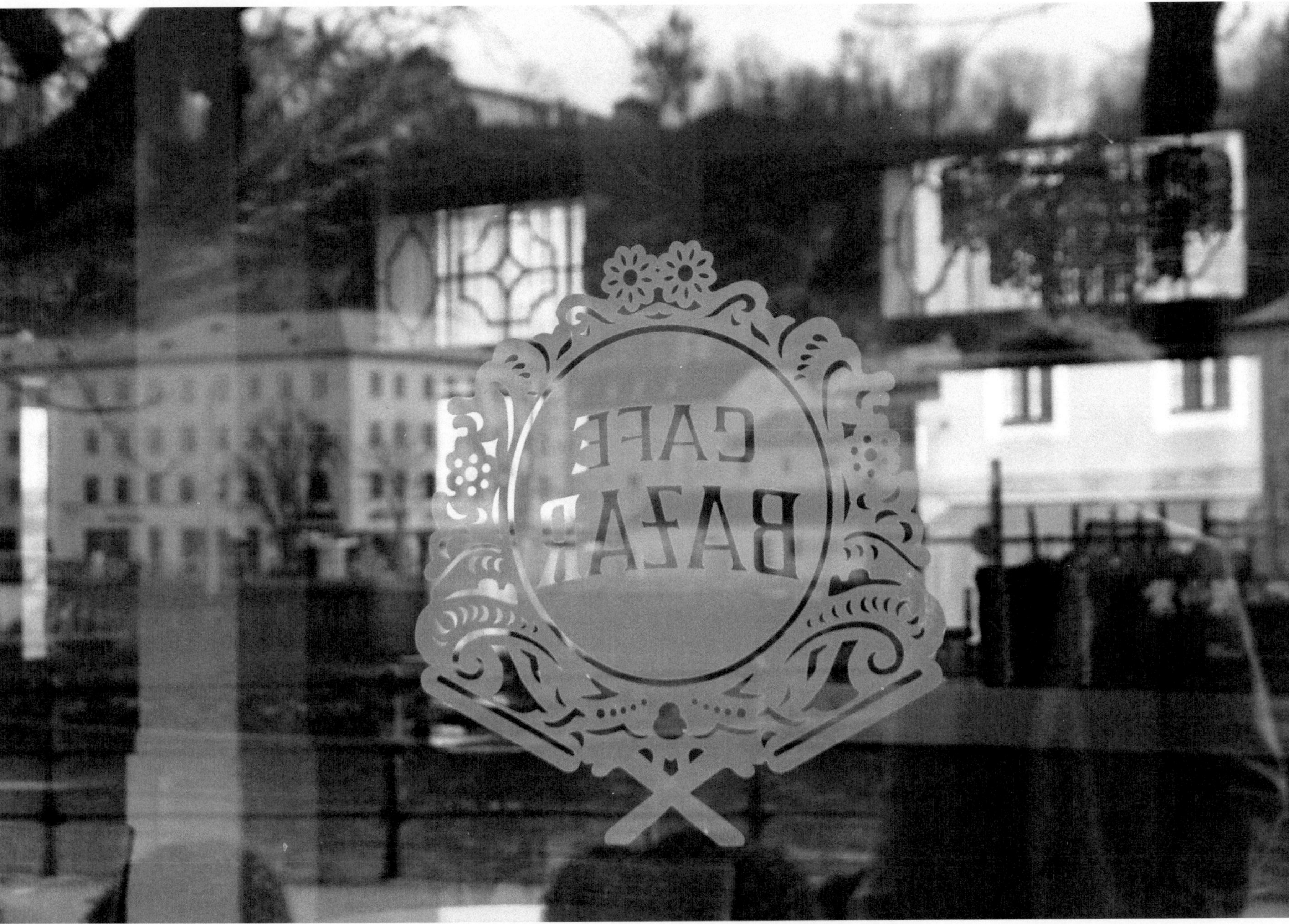

CAFE
BAZAR

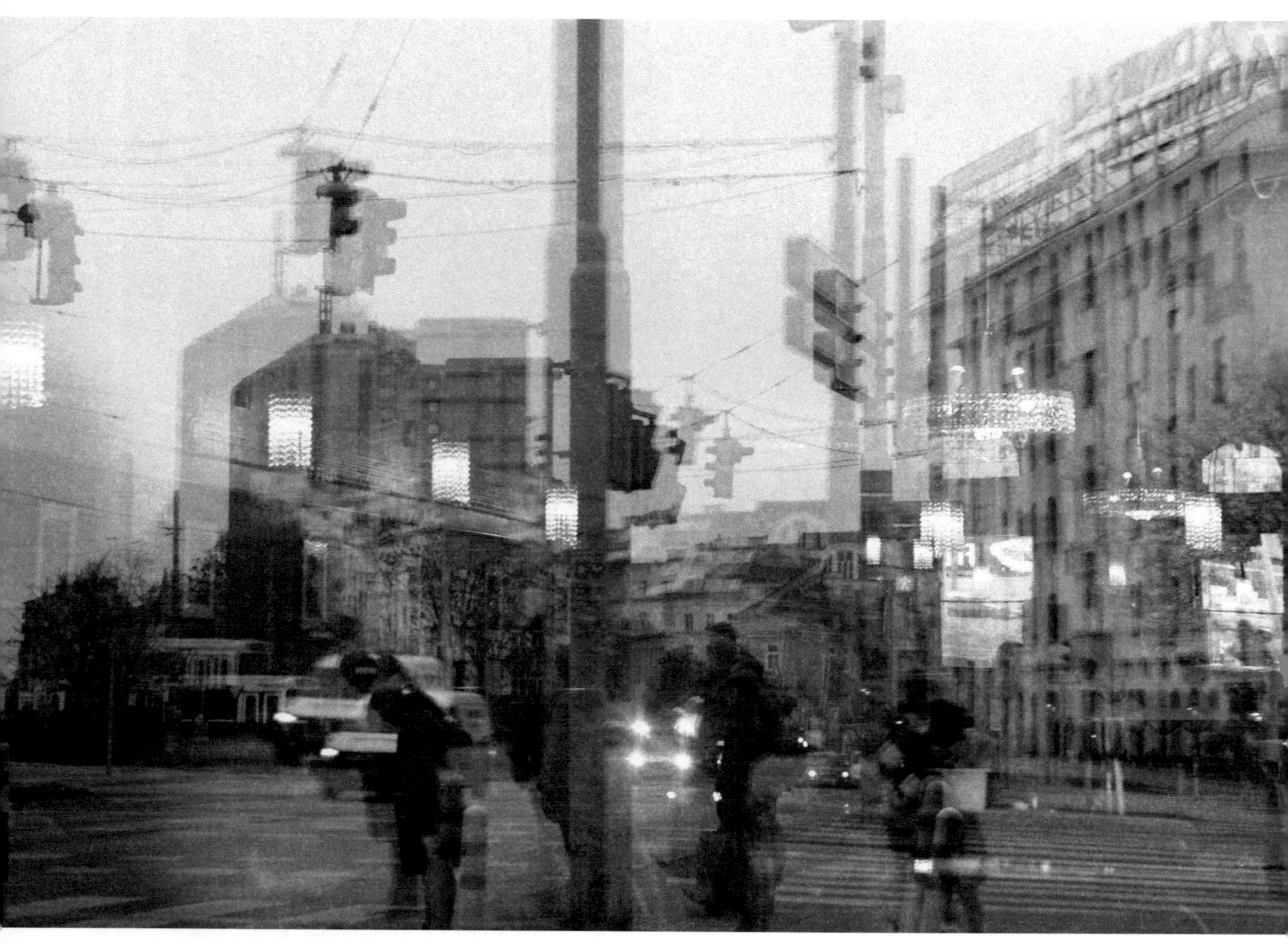

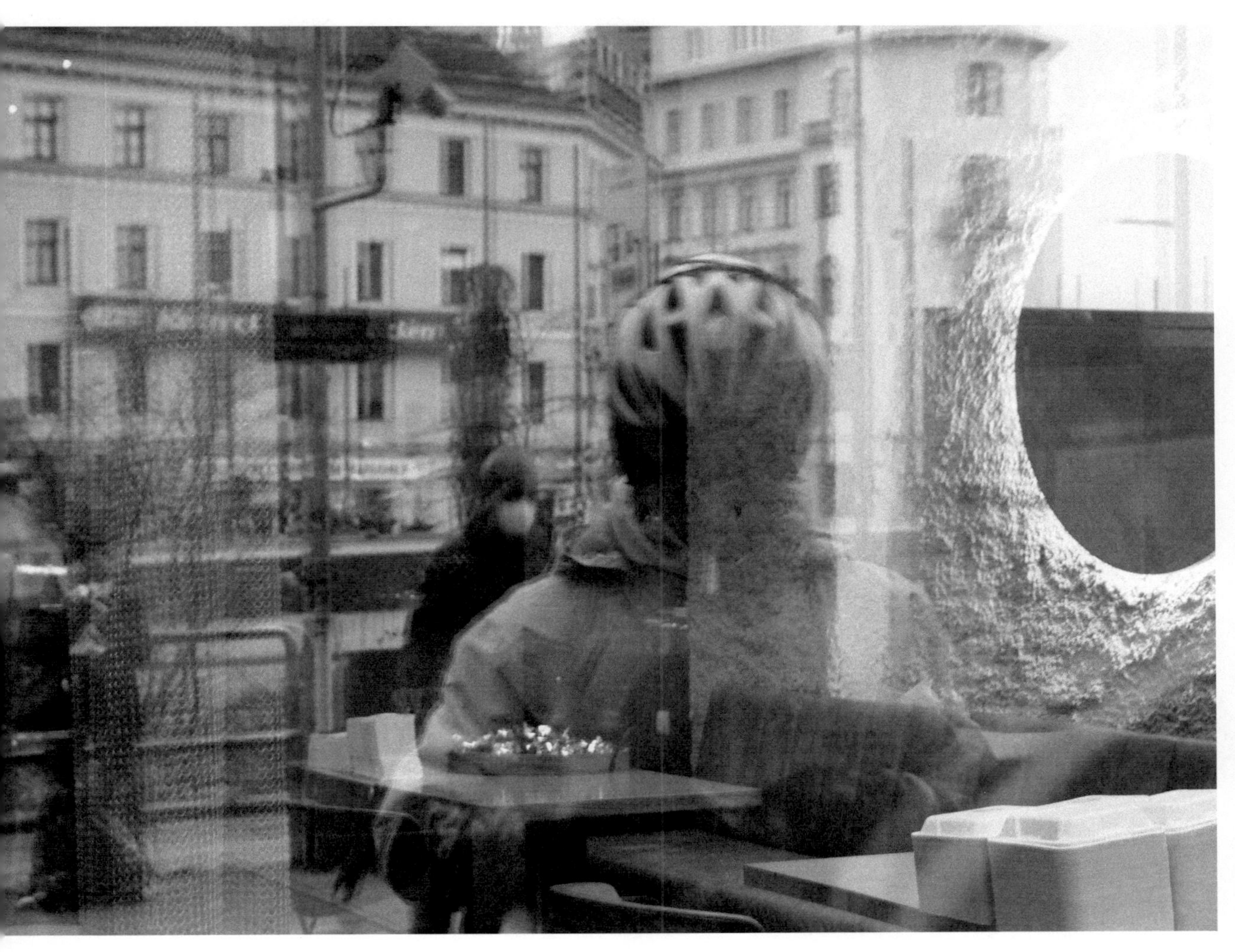